# The Fruit Flavored Family

Garry and Cheryl Baldwin

Parson's Porch Books

*The Fruit Flavored Family*
ISBN: Softcover 978-1-960326-41-6
Copyright © 2023 by Garry and Cheryl Baldwin

**Parson's Porch Books** is an imprint of Parson's Porch *&* Company (PP*&*C) in Cleveland, Tennessee. PP*&*C is a self-funded charity which earns money by publishing books of noted authors, representing all genres. Its face and voice is **David Russell Tullock** (dtullock@parsonsporch.com).

Parson's Porch *&* Company *turns books into bread & milk* by sharing its profits with the poor.

www.parsonsporch.com

*The Fruit Flavored Family*

# Dedication

To our Precious Children, Jeremiah, Anna Grace, and Caleb, whom God used to Grow our Marriage as we Developed our Parenting Skills and to our awesome grandchildren with whom God has continued that development. We love you Ransom, Haven, Nolan, and Grayson. You are the best!

# Contents

# Introduction

*Every Family in the World is Looking
for a Recipe for Success.*

Every family in the world is looking for a way to be happy, content, and valuable. In our ever-changing society the pressure is on to find any way possible to make our families "work". We all want a successful family life. We are looking for answers to all the questions of being a successful husband, wife, parent, and grandparent. We are seeking ways to have a loving, caring, committed family. We want our families to "make it." Everyone is tired of the label "dysfunctional family". People just want this thing called "family" to be functional again. So, what is the recipe for success? What can we do? How can we make the family simple and yet successful?

I remember as a child that my parents wanted what was best for me in all things. When our local pediatrician told my parents that I needed to take a multi-vitamin they bought me the regular ones that tasted terrible. I would hide them or pretend to take them. (I guess that is where my own children got that idea)   Then the maker of multi-vitamins began producing "fruit flavored" ones. I loved them and took them regularly. The fruit flavoring allowed me to get what I needed and to enjoy the taste.

Fruit Flavoring had been around since it was invented by James Van Zandt Blaney, M.D. in 1844, but "the recipe" was only applied to multi-vitamins over a hundred years later. 1

The "fruit flavored" style of leading our families has also been around for many years but is not something that people use. It is a great way to see your family "work". In   a world gone wrong, we have a chance to do what is right. For the Christian believer, the

Holy Spirit in you is this "fruit flavoring". Your love, joy, peace, patience, kindness, goodness, faithfulness, gentleness, and, self-control, placed in you at conversion by the Holy Spirit, is the "fruit flavoring" that allows the family to function smoothly. The overflow of God's Spirit in you "flavors" your parenting and your family with a workable recipe.

This book is the result of years of seeking to be a "fruit flavored" family of faith. Cheryl and I (Garry) have had the honor of being the parents of three children and now the grandparents of four. This is quite a blessing and has allowed us to continue to experience and grow in our lives as a family. So, one can see our parenting journey is well traveled. We are definitely not perfect, but we have been there and love to share.

There is nothing quite like the seeking to apply the experiences of Godly parenting and grandparenting. God has called us to do so, and the rewards are priceless. Cheryl and I have been blessed to "test and approve" many of these Godly truths that you will read about in this book. We have seen them work in the lives of our children and grandchildren. So, after much prompting by friends and fellow parents and grandparents, we have revised an original book we wrote 25 years ago and put down on paper these principles of parenting that have guided us. None of these in and of themselves are perfect and work in every situation.

Children and grandchildren, we have learned, are all individuals and one has to deal with them as such. However, there are many basic principles that work for each and every one. Marriage, parenting, and grand parenting is a work in progress and is always a process. If you seek to do it God's way, it will work.

Let me remind you that this book is not intended to be a guide or a teacher. It is a tool to allow God to speak to you directly and be your guide and teacher. The Holy Spirit is always your teacher in faith and practice. (John 16:13) The Holy Spirit will guide you to understand Truth. Although everyone who reads this book is reading the same words, the Holy Spirit will personalize each chapter to guide each individual toward the lesson he or she needs to learn and apply at this given moment in their lives. As our lives and situations in our families change from day to day, (and for us over the years) may the Holy Spirit bring back to your mind and heart what you will learn during this time you will take to read and study. (John 14:26)

Remember...if you are a believer in the Lord Jesus Christ and know that you have Jesus in your life as your Lord and Savior by faith (Romans 10:9-10; Ephesians 2:8-9; I John 5:11-13) then you can trust God to lead and guide you as a *"fruit flavored family"*. (John 14:7) He wants to make it work through you. He will help you do it.

Finally, as we introduce this writing, never forget that Godly parenting and grandparenting is centered in prayer. It begins there and continues there throughout every task, phase, problem, pain, and victory. Prayer is communicating with God. It is talking to your God and listening to His response. God is always at Work around us and when we "pray without ceasing", God walks and talks with us daily. So we begin this journey with a prayer that God will use this book to speak to your heart.

Your children and grandchildren are watching!

## *"When You Thought I Wasn't Looking"*

When you thought I wasn't looking,
I saw you hang my first painting on the refrigerator,
and I wanted to paint another one.
When you thought I wasn't looking,
I saw you feed a stray cat,
and I thought it was good to be kind to animals.
When you thought I wasn't looking,
I saw you make my favorite cake just for me,
and I knew that little things are special things.
When you thought I wasn't looking,
I heard you say a prayer,
and I believed there is a God I could always talk to.
When you thought I wasn't looking,
I felt you kiss me goodnight, and I felt loved.
When you thought I wasn't looking,
I saw tears come from your eyes,
and I learned that sometimes things hurt,
but it's all right to cry.
When you thought I wasn't looking,
I saw that you cared,
And I wanted to be everything that I could be.
When you thought I wasn't looking,
I looked…and wanted to say thanks for all the things
I saw when you thought, I wasn't looking

-Mary Rita Schilke Korzan

# Family in Crisis

President Theodore Roosevelt in 1917 said:

*"No other success in life--not being President, or being wealthy, or going to college, or anything else--comes up to the success of the men and women who can feel that they have done their duty and that their children and grandchildren rise up to call them blessed."* 2

If you ask any believer in the Lord Jesus Christ what their single most important life ambition is, the majority will say it is to be a Godly person and have a Godly family. We all want to be known as having a "Christian Family". But, in a nation known for Christian values around the world, there is a problem. The Christian family as we know it or think of it is in crisis! Things are not the same!

Years ago, Jean-Marie and Anouk Meyer said: "The crisis of the family is the crisis of society, because without the family there is no social life. The family has its own richness. In the family, each one has value in and of himself. The existence of each person in the family is understood in a logic of love and loyalty, while secularism has no sense of loyalty."3   This "religious realization" is a spiritual reality in our world today. So, the crisis is in our society without a secular cure. The world does not know what to do but recognizes the problem.

A 2022 Gallup poll reported: "A record-high 50% of Americans rate the overall state of moral values in the U.S. as "poor," and another 37% say it is "only fair."

Our society is in a cultural, moral, and spiritual crisis. Is there anything that we can do? We have seen that a political agenda will not work. Public education using "faith based" terminology, has continued for too many years without success. It has not changed. You cannot legislate morality. So what is the solution? How will

God "save America" and all those nations that seek to emulate its system of government. What can we do?

In the morally challenged society of His day, Jesus taught His followers to conduct themselves righteously as they lived and worked among those around them, maintaining moral purity as they awaited His return to affect real, lasting moral renewal. Their cause was to support a proclamation of good news—of the time when His government would bring the change desperately needed by a society in bondage to moral decay. (Matthew 24:14). God has a plan!

Their responsibility, as His (Jesus'), was not to make a political stand but a moral one. With the aid of His precepts, they were to navigate the difficult waters of the moral challenges they and their families would face, while living in a society that often-opposed godly values. This responsibility rests upon individual believers both then and now. This is still His plan.

The Christian family begins with a "Godly" marriage. I must admit that we all have trials and troubles in marriage. Marriage, as an institution, is not perfect, but it is worth the time and effort. What is happening to marriage and the family in 2023?

The first recorded evidence of marriage contracts and ceremonies dates to 4,000 years ago in Mesopotamia. The purpose was the production of heirs, as implied by the Latin word matrimonium, which is derived from "mater" (mother). In ancient Rome, marriage was a civil affair governed by imperial law. But when the empire collapsed, in the 5th century, church courts took over and elevated marriage to a holy union. As the church's power grew through the Middle Ages, so did its influence over marriage. In 1184, marriage was declared as one of the church's seven sacraments and reaffirmed at many of the church councils.[1] But it

---

[1]Francis Schüssler Fiorenza and John P. Galvin, *Systematic Theology: Roman Catholic Perspectives* (Minneapolis: Fortress Press, 1991), 320.

was only in the 16th century that the church allowed public weddings. The Supreme Court of the United States ruled in 1942 saying marriage is "fundamental to the very existence and survival of the human race." This same Supreme Court has applauded the institution of marriage fourteen times since 1888, but it has never clearly defined it. Our secular society is moving toward a new definition of marriage. This definition is from the created morals of human preferences and desires without regard to culture. It is based on simply a relationship between two people. So our society says whether it is one man and one woman or a same-sex couple, marriage is a relational institution. Sharon Jayson of USA today wrote, "America appears to have fallen out of love with marriage." With all the debate and lack of acceptance of "absolute Truth," the changing views of marriage show "today's Americans are less likely to be hitched than any generation before them."[2] As a result, in the 1980's only 13% of children were born outside of marriage. Today it is about 40%. In the 1960's "divorce posed the greatest threat to the family, but now it is co-habituating households with children which threatens the quality and stability of children's lives (and the family) in today's society."[3] And the Christian's defense fund even echoed, "one in two children will live in a single-parent family at some point."[4] So we have personal choices to make!

**We, as individuals, must accept our personal responsibility for our own families!**

---

[2]*Elizabeth Marquardt, David Blankenhorn, Robert* I. Lerman, Linda Malone-Colón, and W. Bradford Wilcox, "The President's Marriage Agenda for the Forgotten Sixty Percent," The State of Our Unions (Charlottesville, VA: National Marriage Project and Institute for American Values, 2012), 62.

[3]Ibid, 87.

[4]Children's Defense Fund (2012), State of Americas Children: 2012, Washington, DC; Children's Defense Fund, 1.

What are we talking about anyway? What are common traits of a healthy and wholesome family? The basics never change. Psychologist Dolores Curran conducted a survey of 551 professionals who are involved with family matters, and she came up with the following fifteen common traits of families who tend to be happy and harmonious: She concluded, and we agree:

The Healthy Family:

1. Communicates and listens
2. Affirms and supports one another
3. Teaches respect for others
4. Develops a sense of trust
5. Has a sense of play and humor
6. Exhibits a sense of shared responsibility
7. Teaches a sense of right and wrong
8. Has a strong sense of family in which rituals and traditions abound
9. Has a balance of interaction among members
10. Has a shared religious core
11. Respects the privacy of one another
12. Values service to others
13 Fosters family table time and conversation
14. Shares leisure time
15. Admits to and seeks help with problems.[5]

If even the world's research and surveys see these as the target areas that seem to be the goal of successful parenting, how does one get the training? We are so glad you asked, and this is the purpose of this book.

God has uniquely gifted the believer to lead the family by example. There is no reason why the family should not be super-successful in every area and in all ways. There are plenty of reasons why we can begin to restore our values to Godly standards. These standards will allow the family to truly be happy, healthy, and harmonious. Even though meeting the needs of the family may seem like a balancing act at times, the Lord has filled His believers with the power and the potential to accomplish it.

**We just need to learn to Apply and Exemplify, so we can Amplify the "Fruit Flavored Family".**

The Apostle Paul spoke of this truth when he wrote in Galatians 5:22-23:

*"But the fruit of the Spirit is love, joy, peace, patience, kindness, goodness, faithfulness, gentleness and self-control. Against such things there is no law"*
*..NIV*

If we will draw from God's Word in these verses in Galatians to develop some time-tested Biblical principles, then the Holy Spirit will guide and teach us to understand and learn how to apply them.

*Let's begin by defining the term*

### *"Fruit Flavored Family".*

The "fruit flavored" style (traditional, biblical) of leading our families has been around for many years but is not something that people use. It is a great way to see your family "work" but must be worked on and lived out by the power of the Holy Spirit in you. In a world gone wrong, we have a chance to do what is right. For the Christian believer, the Holy Spirit in you is this "fruit flavoring". Your love, joy, peace, patience, kindness, goodness, faithfulness, gentleness, and self-control is the "fruit flavoring" that allows the family to function smoothly. The overflow of God's Spirit in you "flavors" your parenting and your family. We can live this out personally in our families. It is our prayer that this book would be used to help those who are struggling in their families or those who want to fine tune their family. We know, by experience, that it is tough to go through the day to day challenges of being a Godly family. We want to help you by sharing with you that with God all things are possible.

# Discovering Your Families Uniqueness

We want to insert a chapter that will set a practical foundation for communication and instruction within your family at all ages. It is something that has been very helpful for us over the years. Take time to read it over several times. It may look difficult, but it really is not. We have found that it is so very helpful in discovering how each person in your family relates to one another.

Every child is different! If you are a parent or grandparent you already know that. But, there are some basic personality traits that are present in all children and can help us in "raising" them.

These traits can allow us to go crazy or be successful in parenting and/or grandparenting.

Cheryl and I have **disc**overed that by **disc**erning these traits we can literally **disc**iple our children and grandchildren. (catch the **disc** play on words)

Proverbs 22:6 says:

*Train up a child in the way he should go; even when he is old he will not depart from it.*

*The original Hebrew language in which this was written in the Bible would translate this text with a little more explanation. It would say, (our translation) Train (Parent, Disciple) a child according to their personality blend in order to understand key truths about them and them way of learning and growing mentally and emotionally and when they are old they will be mature and able to understand absolute truth.*

When God gives you Discernment to Discover some common sense or behavioral knowledge about your children, it is to prepare you to Disciple (to train them). God is at work in every life, and He is wanting to use you to "do" His Will as a parent and a grandparent. It is your responsibility! "God does not eliminate your knowledge or common sense, He consecrates it, and gives you wisdom to understand and to obey and apply His will and ways. (Is. 55:8-9). This is why we all have unique personalities.

All children are wonderful and unique in their personality! Have you discovered that already? And…God has assigned you the awesome task to train up your children according to their personality in order for them to be fruitful in their calling in life! Wow! Now How? How can we learn to be used of God in the process? By understanding basic personality traits!

What is a Personality? It is how we perceive things…(using our senses and intuition), How we make decisions (objectively and subjectively), It orders our preferences…It displays our behavior. Behavioral Personality traits are developed by nature and nurture.

Active, Passive, Task or People oriented dominant and secondary. As one writer put it: *"What makes people tick and what ticks them off."* Understanding why people respond and react the way they do. Let us introduce you to a simple way to do that.

The **DISC** Model of Human Behavior was first introduced as the 4 Temperament Types by Hippocrates 400 years before Christ. It identified four classic types: Choleric, Sanguine, Phlegmatic, and Melancholy Types to describe human behavior and personality insights. In 1929, William Marston changed the old Greek titles to: Dominant, Inspirational, Submissive, and Compliant. Then in 1943 Katherine Briggs, and her daughter Isabelle Briggs Meyers introduced a more complicated and deeper profile called the MBTI (16 types…blends)

The DISC Personality Types is now perhaps the most popular of all the models. Dr. Mels Carbonell created one of the most comprehensive online DISC computer profiles. Dr. John Geier created the first paper instrument, the *Performax Personal Profile*

*System* in 1977. Dr. Carbonell, who I studied under, was the first to combine Spiritual Gifts with the 4 DISC Personality Types. Most problems are personality problems, which is understanding and learning how to communicate with one another. So we must understand how people look at and understand what is going on Personally. Below is a summary of the DISC types of Personality function:

### D- Outgoing...Task Oriented

*(Dominant, Direct, Demanding, Decisive, Determined)*

*This trait describes the way you deal with problems, assert yourself and control situations.*

### I- Outgoing...People Oriented

*(Inspiring, Influencing, Impressing, Inducing)*

*This trait describes the way you deal with people, the way you communicate and relate to others.*

### S- Reserved...People Oriented

*(Submissive, Steady, Stable, Security-oriented)   This trait describes your temperament, patient, persistent, and thoughtful in most situations.*

### C- Reserved...Task Oriented

*(Competent, Compliant, Cautious, Calculating) This trait describes how you approach and organize your activity, procedures, and responsibilities.*

### DISC Patterns or Profiles

As you will appreciate, there are literally thousands of different combinations of scores. Therefore to help interpretation, communication and understanding, DISC Personality Model experts have defined - through statistical analysis of the score combinations - fifteen DISC 'Patterns' or 'Profiles'. The 'Profiles' are often given names. The objective of these names is to give a single descriptive term that captures the essence of that Profile. Names often used are Achiever, Coach, Evaluator, Counselor,

Creative, Individualist, Inspirational, Investigator, Objective Thinker, Perfectionist, Persuader, Practitioner, Enthusiast, Results-Oriented or Specialist

To understand the DISC theory even further descriptions are given for people who score comparatively high and comparatively low on each of the four DISC dimensions:

## Dominance...Comparatively High

- enjoys competition and challenge.
- Is goal orientated and want to be recognized for their efforts.
- aim high, want authority and are generally resourceful and adaptable.
- are usually self-sufficient and individualistic.
- may lose interest in projects once the challenge has gone and they tend to be impatient and dissatisfied with minor detail.

They are usually direct and positive with people, enjoying being the center of attraction and may take it for granted that people will think highly of them. They may have a tendency to be rather critical of others. Consequently, other people may tend to see them as being rather domineering and overpowering.

## *Dominance ...Comparatively Low*

- tend to want peace and harmony.
- prefer to let others initiate action and resolve problems.
- are quiet and indirect in their approach to most situations.
- are usually cautious and calculate risks carefully before acting.
- They are generally well liked because of their mild and gentle nature. Other people will tend to see them as being patient, calm, thoughtful and a good listener.

## Influence...Comparatively High

- are strongly interested in meeting and being with people.

- are generally optimistic, outgoing, and socially skilled.
- are quick at establishing relationships.
- Sometimes their concern for people and people's feelings may make them reluctant to disturb a favorable situation or relationship.

## Influence...Comparatively Low

- are usually socially passive.
- quite frequently have an affinity for things, machinery and equipment.
- are generally comfortable working alone.
- frequently have a tendency to be analytical and once they have sorted the facts out they communicate them in a straightforward direct way.
- tend to take little at face value.
- They may well have learned and developed good social skills, but they only bring these into play when logic dictates such tactics.

## Steadiness...Comparatively High

- are usually patient, calm and controlled.
- have a high willingness to help others particularly those they consider as friends.
- Generally they have the ability to deal with the task in hand and to do routine work with patience and care.

## Steadiness...Comparatively Low

- tends to enjoy change and variety in their work and non-work life.
- are expansive by nature and tend not to like routine and repetitive work/activities.
- They enjoy stretching themselves intellectually and physically.

## Compliance...Comparatively High

- are usually peaceful and adaptable.
- tend not to be aggressive.

- tend to be cautious rather than impulsive.
- avoid risk-taking.
- act in a tactful, diplomatic way and strive for a stable, ordered life.
- are comfortable following procedures in both their personal and business life.
- They prefer sticking to methods that have proved successful in the past. They have a high acceptance of rules and regulations.

## Compliance...Comparatively Low

- are independent and uninhibited.
- resent rules and restrictions.
- prefer to be measured by results and are always willing to try the untried.
  - Free in thought, word and deed, they long for freedom and go to great lengths to achieve it. They feel that repetitive detail and routine work is best "delegated" or avoided.

## *Personal Application*

Now, let us suggest you try something. Go to Take the Test online for free: https://www.123test.com/disc-personality-test/

Take the test and learn your own personality and how you respond and react to others. Then take the test for your children or grandchildren by thinking about what you have observed in their personalities and how they respond and react. Now these results are not perfect, but we have found are a pretty good indicator of what yours and their personality might be. This is simply an introduction, and you can purchase more on the subject by looking at: Uniquelyyou.org

# Preparing for the Production

*"There is no doubt that around the family and the home*
*that all the greatest virtues, the most dominating virtues of*
*human society, are created, strengthened, and maintained"*
…..Winston Churchhill 6

Have you known the agony of not doing the right thing?
Have you ever thought, "I ought to do this or that" only to forget
all about it? Have you ever promised yourself that you'll never say
something or do something only to blurt it out or do it anyway?
Have you ever thought, "I can't change – I'll always act like this"?
Have you fallen into the trap of comparing yourself to others?
Have you ever thought, "At least I'm not like that guy down the
street"? Have you consoled yourself about your failures and
shortcomings by making a list of the obviously huge sins of others?
In the middle of comparing yourself to others have you ever
thrown your hands up in despair and said, "I really am no good"?
If you have asked yourself these questions and wondered, like me,
What is my problem, I need to do something, then read on please.
Most family problems have been experienced and solved some
time before you or I existed. Most situations and circumstances
that we experience in our daily family existence are common and
simple to take care of. However, when it is our first time as a
parent, and we don't want to be embarrassed and ask anyone for
help, we struggle to make it. You may be thinking, "I've tried
before in my family, I don't know how and don't think I can." Left
to ourselves, we cannot make all the changes we need to make. On
our own we cannot keep on doing all that we should do. Let's face
it, our lives are beyond our control. Without help, we usually will
fail to do the right thing. But we are not alone…God's people have
not CHANGED in thousands of years. In fact, the Jewish
prophets described the people of their time as GRAPEVINES
gone wild…

Isaiah said… "I will sing for the one I love a song about his vineyard: My loved one had a vineyard on a fertile hillside. He dug it up and cleared it of stones and planted it with the choicest vines. He built a watchtower in it and cut out a winepress as well. Then he looked for a crop of good grapes, but it yielded only bad fruit (Isaiah 5:1-2 NIV)."

Jeremiah passed along God's word to the people when he wrote; "I had planted you like a choice vine of sound and reliable stock. How then did you turn against me into a corrupt, wild vine?" (Jeremiah 2:21 NIV).

But Jesus came with a new message about the God's grapevine…"I am the true vine, and my Father is the gardener…(John 15:1-17)

You can make changes in your family!

### LESSONS FROM A SCUPPERNONG VINE

Growing up in Burlington, North Carolina, we had a Scuppernong Vine (like a wild grape) that belonged to a neighbor right along our property line. The man wanted to cut it down, Dad talked him into giving it to us and began to attend to it… Most fruit vines would rather produce shoots and leaves than fruits. They end up looking lush and green, but ultimately they are only good for making decorations. Scuppernong vines are the same. Like most fruit vines, they also must be pruned radically. The gardener must be vigilant, cutting them back each year as far as he possibly can. Branches with no fruit must be removed so they don't draw nutrients away from the other fruit. And fruitful branches must be pruned back to produce even more in the following year. Only if you do this with total commitment will you produce fruit. It takes work. And if you can keep your kids away from eating all the fruit before you harvest it, you will have a good crop.

What we learn about fruit vines and how that message from Jesus pertains to us, gives us hope. We can work and see fruit produced in our family. (My dad knew this also)

It teaches us that God doesn't want to leave us on our own. He wants to be the Gardner who cares for us and makes us fruitful. It reveals to us that God is at work in our lives. It tells us that God can do in us and through us what we could never do by ourselves. It tells us that He will make us more and more fruitful – giving us more and more righteous attitudes and actions. It tells us that Jesus Himself will live in us and God will answer our prayers as we learn to put the Bible into practice. The Bible teaches us these truths quite clearly. You see, this is what this passage in John 15 is all about. (Read John 15 in the Bible and then read on in the book)

In John 15, God as the Great Gardener, and Christ as the Excellent Vine, wants us to remain in the vineyard to produce good fruit. Again, please do not forget that we are talking about the Fruit Flavored Family with this example. Remaining and bearing are the two interwoven themes we're going to look at a little closer. These two themes "are" closely related because it is only when we abide in Christ that we can truly bear fruit. If we do not abide in Christ we cannot bear fruit and therefore, according to Jesus' words, we will be cut off from the vine. This is the basics of marriage and family growth. God is at work in our lives! He wants us to be fruitful and multiply. (Genesis 1:28) Remain (abide) in Me, and I in you. Did you know that the word "remain" or "abide" occurs no less than six times in chapter 15 of John's Gospel? In answering the question, "How do we make this "remaining" process happen, this passage provides clues from Jesus Himself." The word remain (abide) simply means to live. In order to have a fruitful marriage and family our lives must be centered in the Lord Jesus Christ. Now How?

1. *Feed ourselves with the words of Jesus:* Again: "If you abide in Me, and my words abide in you, ask whatever you will, and it shall be done for you." The words of Jesus are life. They are the sap that flows from the root up into the branches.

PSALM 1 says…"Blessed is the one whose delight is in the law of the LORD, and on His law they meditate day and night. They are like a tree planted by streams of water that yields its fruit in its season; its leaf does not wither. In all that they do, they prosper."

In order to remain (live, abide and prosper), we need to feed ourselves on God's word. Take time to read it.

2. *We also need to feed ourselves with an active prayer life.* (John 15:7) This follows from remaining in God's word. Verse 7 says, "If you remain in Me and My words remain in you, ask and whatever you wish will be given." In order to remain, we need to have an active prayer life.

3. *We also need to feed ourselves by showing love to others.* (John 15:9-15 & 13:35) In v. 8, Jesus says that in remaining we will be "showing ourselves to be (His) disciples." How do we show ourselves? Look at verse 9 and following…its love! No surprise here. In order to remain, we need to show love to others. You see when you apply God's Word, you develop God's Truth within you. But maybe remaining isn't your problem. You've accepted Christ and all He promised. You study enough Bible to get by and love your neighbors most of the time. But are you bearing fruit or are you withering? Is your family fruit flavored? Do you meet with God out of habit or out of love?

Some of us get so busy that we miss out on the things God is saying to us. When our "busyness" interferes with our relationship with God then that relationship will wither. If we ever find excuses for not spending time in prayer, or spending time reading the Bible, or being together as God's family, then we're too busy to foster good fruit.

It becomes essential, then in beginning the process of Marriage and Family enrichment to take a good honest look at yourself and your family. When we decide to make our family more fruitful, we can be assured that this is God's desire also. He wants His creation to be fruitful and multiply. He wants us to be successful and prosperous. He wants us to produce more fruit… much fruit. Over and over again God has made this a reality in so many lives. When we as Parents and Grandparents make this decision to tend to "our" grapevines of faith and character we are producing a lasting legacy of fruit production. Grapevines can grow for over 120 years we are told. That is your families lifetimes. Let's all tend to our "vines" and produce "much fruit" showing ourselves to be His Disciple.

And now it's your turn.

# Identity and Destiny

We have covered a lot of territory in these first two chapters. We have defined our purpose, we have looked at "remaining" (really living) ...the need we have as Christians to feed ourselves on the Word, on an active prayer life, and by showing love to others. We have looked at fruit development.

In fact, there are only two kinds of fruit that our lives can produce. (bad or good) On the one hand, all by ourselves, we can produce every type of sin imaginable (bad fruit) and on the other, with God's help, we can produce the attitudes and actions of Christ in all that we do. (good fruit)

There is a story that is told about a retired teacher, an elderly man who lived alone in a small town and was well known for his wisdom and his knowledge and ability to quiet smart remarks of his students. One day a group of former students decided they would play a trick on this wise old man at the expense of a small bird. They came up with this plan. They would go to the man and say, "We have a bird in our hands, is it alive or dead?" If the man said dead, they would open their hands and let it go, if he said alive, they would crush the bird and reveal it was dead. He could not get it right. And so the day came, and the students went to the man's home. "Wise old man, they said, we have a bird in our hands, is it alive or dead?" The man paused, thought carefully and responded: "That choice is in your hands..."

**And so it is with fruit production:** *God has left the decision in our hands. Either we'll keep on depending on our own abilities, or we will turn to Christ to do what we could never do alone. He is the True Vine and gives us a choice. Praise be to God.*

29

*John 15:8 "By this My Father is glorified, that you bear much fruit; so you will be My disciples."*

*Matthew 5:16 "Let your light so shine before men, that they may see your good works and glorify your Father in heaven."*

As one brother said it: "Let your big, juicy grapes be seen of all men, so that they may glorify the Gardener by coming to know Him as you do!."

Pray with me as we begin this chapter: Heavenly Father, We come to You knowing our limitations. We come to You knowing Your promises. We come to You knowing that now is the time to ask for Your assistance in our fruit production. May Your Word challenge us to be all that You would have us to be. May Your Holy Spirit guide and direct us, as we know we cannot do this on our own. And may the One who redeemed and saved us, remain in us always, so that we may become the best fruit producers for Christ as we remain in Him. Help us to stay close to these promises. Help us when we fail, to not get discouraged. Help us when we win, to give You all the glory. Help us to depend on You, through Your Son Jesus Christ, and the sustaining nature of Your Spirit, we pray...Amen

**Seeking to become "the fruit flavored family" takes work and effort. Let us again remind you of these fruits in Galatians 5:22-23:**

*"But the fruit of the Spirit is love, joy, peace, patience, kindness, goodness, faithfulness, gentleness and self-control. Against such things there is no law"...NIV*

Let's continue to use these nine (9) fruits of the Spirit found in this text and examine how we can utilize what the Father has already placed within us by His Holy Spirit to do so. Using examples from God's Word and personal experience let's develop a plan to lead our family with a "family first" mentality. Can you do it?

***You can if you think you can!***

I just Love chocolate chip cookies. I like the soft chewy kind, where they use Hershey's Kisses for chocolate chips. My great aunt, Josie, would make every time that Frankie, my cousin and I would come to see her. When we were around 6 or 7 on our way to visit our grandmother, lovingly called, Maw-Maw, we would stop by Josie's house, just to get those cookies. In order to get to Josie's house from Maw-Maws, one had to travel about a mile down the road or, you could take a shortcut across the graveyard and get there in about one third of the time. So most of the time we would always take the shortcut for we figured we could outrun most booger men. This particular day it got dark earlier than we expected. We also did not know they had dug a fresh grave in the cemetery we ran through as a shortcut. Now in that part of the country they dug graves deep so the dead couldn't or wouldn't get out, about 7 or 8 feet deep. Josie told us that she was making a fresh batch of cookies, and so Frankie and I decided one of us should go on to Maw-Maws so we wouldn't get it trouble for not being on time. Frankie took off first, and I would follow later with the cookies.

As Frankie ran to the graveyard, he fell in the grave that was open all the way to the bottom of it. Screaming and hollering as he hit, he tried frantically to get out, climbing up the sides but falling back down. And so after a few minutes of trying without success, he came to the conclusion that he would have to spend the night in the grave. After a few minutes, with cookies in hand I was ready to leave. I had to make a decision how I was going to Maw-Maw's. I could go the mile down the road or cut across the graveyard. I too figured I could outrun most booger men, so I took off running. I ran, oh so fast till I ran into the open grave. Screaming and hollering, I tried my best to get out of the grave, climbing up the sides, but falling down, jumping and seeking to get out, until I came to the conclusion that I would have to spend the night in the grave. Remember Frankie; he has been sitting there in the corner watching this the whole time. Until now, he had not said a word, but then he uttered 7 words that changed my life… He said, "You will never get out of here", but I did with one leap. I was out of the grave.

*You can, if you think you can and if the motivation is right.*

We've all heard that life is to be…God First (Personal), Family Second, and Ministry Third. Sounds good, but How can one do it?

The evidence that this is a reality is in the fruit.

Jesus said, "you will know my disciples by their fruit", and so Paul is saying here in Galatians 5 that the fruit of the spirit is found in these characteristics. These virtues are character traits that are within just waiting to be developed and manifested, so let's begin and see how.

Many, many years ago, I took my son who was 16 at the time on a "rite of passage" retreat. The Belgian anthropologist Arnold van Gennep coined the phrase rite of passage in 1909 to explain the process people of many different cultures experience in moving from one stage in life to another. In coming of age, the experience is marked by two transitions: one from childhood to adolescence and another from adolescence to adulthood.

Around the time of Jesus' birth, Jewish males were reading and memorizing the *Torah* (first five books of the Old Testament, also known as "the law") at an early age. At ten, Jewish males were learning the *Mishnah*. (the Oral law of the Jewish nation) At 13, they were "bound" to the commandments, and at 15, they studied the *Talmud* (Customs and History of the Jewish nation). It was an honor to study the Torah and teach it. Becoming a rabbi was one of the greatest privileges, callings, and honors to receive.

Luke 2:42-52 records Jesus going to Jerusalem with His parents. Every adult male living within 15 miles of Jerusalem was expected to attend the Passover festival. A Jewish boy became a man at 12 years old, so you can imagine the excitement Jesus must have been feeling while journeying to Jerusalem. This was certainly a rite of passage for Him, or at least a taste of great things to come. When the Passover was over, Mary and Joseph headed home, each one thinking that Jesus was with the other, since the men and women usually traveled separately in caravans. When Mary and Joseph realized He wasn't with them and they returned to Jerusalem, they found Jesus where one would not expect a 12-year-old male of His day to be—in the temple. What was Jesus doing? Sitting "among the teachers [rabbis], listening to them, and asking questions." What were the rabbis thinking? They were "all quite taken with Him, impressed with the sharpness of His answers." At 13, a Jewish boy became a *bar mitzvah*, "son of the law," in which he entered into full adulthood.

For me, my son's "rite of passage" was in order to provide a formal time of training and guidance on the basics of manhood while keeping it in an informal setting. I focused on 2 terms in order to help him move into the identification (I.D.) of manhood.

### *Identity and Destiny...*

I wanted his identification to be defined by understanding his identity and his destiny. By Identity I meant...Who he was in himself and then who he was in Christ (Value) By Destiny I meant...Why God saved him and Where he could choose to go, or how he could follow Christ. (Vision) A big part of the reason this made sense was in the development of our relationship over the years. I had begun to develop a relationship with my son from the time of his birth in order to know and impart wisdom to him. I wanted to bless my son, but my father had never "Biblically" blessed me, so I had to learn and share from my Heavenly Father. I wanted this to be our Legacy: **Being Blessed and Blessing our families.** By blessing I mean a meaningful touch, or a spoken message that attaches value and vision to the one being blessed. It comes from the Hebrew word *Baruch* which means to empower to prosper. It is one of the most important words in the Bible used over 640 times in the Old Testament alone.

Its purpose was to clarify direction in life, unify the purpose of life, provide protection from life, and to help in the growth and maturity process. Simply put, to bless was to provide significance and security (worth and wisdom).

God's nature is to bless, and nothing is greater than God's nature, therefore, whatever comes your way, can be a pathway toward a blessing from God. What a special gift... To know that God wants to give you a blessing.

In the Old Testament, a father would bless his children by laying their hands upon them and saying messages of support and encouragement. Giving direction, purpose, and protection. We must see all that happens to us as a blessing...the hand of God upon us and share those truths with our children and grandchildren. To bless in the biblical sense is to ask for divine favor. We are asking God to direct our paths and trusting Him to do it. When we ask for God's blessing, we're not asking for more of what we could get for ourselves. We are crying out to God for His wonderful, unlimited goodness. This is what the writer in Proverbs was referring to when he said in Proverbs 10:22... *"The blessing of the LORD brings wealth, and He adds no trouble to it."* When God's blessings finds no obstructions in you, nothing to stop them, you will become a conduit of blessings for yourself and others...All things will work together for the good in your life....You will be blessed...and able to bless.

I am appointed by God to be an active part of that blessing in order to make the blessing become reality. This is why my son and I cover these truths as father and son in the light of fruit flavored reality. In other words in a taste he could handle and accept as real. One final part of this was to use this "blessing" at my oldest son's wedding preparation time. We gathered as a family to speak words of blessing to him. Each adult male in our family, spoke these words to Jeremiah (our oldest). And we did the same at our youngest son Caleb's wedding.

I want to add one most important and sometimes overlooked giving of blessings also. You see in the middle of my 2 boys, I was blessed with a girl. Cheryl went through the same material covered above with a trip with our daughter Anna Grace. It was a special mother/daughter time covering the same basic material I covered with the boys, but specific to the life of a Godly woman. In Jewish history this is called a "bat mitzpah" meaning "a daughter of the commandment". Don't see God's Word as "sexist". God set a basic pattern for life, and we need to follow it. We cannot let the ways of our world and the thoughts of man to discount or discredit the infallible Word of God. God's value for man and woman is equal. Each of us have a role and a responsibility that we must learn and live out for our children and grandchildren's sake.

*So, can we do the same thing as Husbands, Wives Parents, and Grandparents, and maybe discover our own identity, destiny, and legacy of blessing? Yes we can, Let's learn how!*

*In this next section, we are going to look at each of the 9 fruits of the Spirit in detail with example of application. This is the beginning of doing and being the "Fruit Flavored Family" of faith. You must accept God's Love as your own and ask the LORD to live these out in your life. And you must be obedient to His Word and His Ways. So let's learn how. If you have asked Jesus to be your LORD and Savior, repented of your sins and are wanting Jesus to take control of your life, He will. Right now, just say, "Help me LORD!"*

# Love

Greek - *Agape*
(charity, benevolent affection and care)

The 13th chapter of 1 Corinthians is probably one of the most familiar of all scriptures. Some have said that this chapter is the greatest, strongest, and deepest thing that the apostle Paul ever penned. It has been called the hymn of love. It is a unique chapter.

What is love anyway? What are we talking about? I mean many of us can use the word Love and it mean different things. I love my wife, but I also love fried chicken. Is that the same? Well if I want to compare Cheryl to a greasy bird it is…but I don't think so. Paul is using the Greek word Agape here, which is the highest level of love. Several other words are used for love in the Greek and in our language. We're not talking about romantic, emotional, brotherly love or the love of an object, but this love is the act of commitment and self-sacrifice. This is the love God demonstrated when He became a man and died for our sin. It is love that is action oriented. It is love that is humble, meeting needs, and doing what God wants us to do. It's the love God wants His church to demonstrate to the World. It is the love we all need to learn. It is the love parents and grandparents must naturally share with our family.

Can we understand this love and apply it to our lives? Let's look closely at 1 Corinthians 13 and see if we can learn what love is and how to put this love into practice.

It is sad to say that as urgent, as important, and divine as love is, it is frequently missing from the church and our families. I mean, we can teach, help people, and give money without any love at all. You can give without loving, but you can't live without giving. This was Paul's point. So He defines love vividly in 1 Corinthians 13 v. 1-3

*If I speak in the tongues of men or of angels, but do not have love, I am only a resounding gong or a clanging cymbal.* ²*If I have the gift of prophecy and can fathom all mysteries and all knowledge, and if I have a faith that can move mountains, but do not have love, I am nothing.* ³*If I give all I possess to the poor and give over my body to hardship that I may boast, but do not have love I gain nothing.*

1. Love is Defined…

Love is represented in the Scriptures as an attribute of God and as a Christian virtue. It is seen in both theology and ethics. Love is the highest characteristic of God when we see it demonstrated in the life of individuals. Christian Love is seen in the overflow of God's affection through us. For example in the 105 verses in 1 John, love is mentioned more than forty times to define what true love looks like.

Love starts and stops with God. He is the Author. He created it out of His very nature, and He desires that we share and experience this wonderful gift to humankind. I think it is interesting to compare the most familiar verse in the Bible with another verse that John wrote. Most people can quote John 3:16 but look at 1 John 3:16: *"By this we know love, because He laid down His life for us. And we also ought to lay down our lives for the brethren."* I understand that the numbers or references on the verses are not in the original Greek writing, but the two 3:16 verses have a complementary message: love gives sacrificially. The world knows little about sacrificial love. God is love and clearly shows us it's definition by demonstrating this wonderful gift. (Romans 5:8)

So….LOVE is an outflow of the Holy Spirit. God wants to love through us as He lives within us.

Love is the action of doing what is best for someone. Paul wanted the Corinthians to understand that agape love is a necessary reality of being a believer. He wanted them to realize that love plays a prominent part in all Christian behavior, and without it, the behavior ceases to be Christian. Notice He uses the word "I" in v. 1-3, so it is up to individuals. It's up to you and me. God wants us to be Agape love…So the chapter continues as

2. Love is Described… Paul describes love in v. 4-8…

*⁴Love is patient, love is kind. It does not envy, it does not boast, it is not proud. ⁵It does not dishonor others, it is not self-seeking, it is not easily angered, it keeps no record of wrongs. ⁶Love does not delight in evil but rejoices with the truth. ⁷It always protects, always trusts, always hopes, always perseveres. ⁸Love never fails. But where there are prophecies, they will cease; where there are tongues, they will be stilled; where there is knowledge, it will pass away.*

The entire description is in terms of behavior, things we need to live out. Now Paul's description of love is not a list of things you and I don't understand, they are actually things we know and want to do, but do not take the time to do them. *Love is action oriented*…doing what is right.

It is important to understand that the portrait Paul is presenting is in contrast to the behavior of the Corinthians. They didn't have love, and were actually the opposite of love, so Paul had to describe love's behavior to them. I'm afraid, however, that we are no better. We all need to hear what Paul is saying and examine our own lives. Our children and grandchildren need to see that love demonstrated so we must examine ourselves.

Basically what Paul is saying is this…Agape Love is very patient, but we are mostly impatient. Love is very kind, but we are frequently unkind. Love knows no jealousy, but we are often jealous. Love makes no parade, but we are proud…and on and on. That's Paul's approach. He is putting all the positives of love against the negatives of the Corinthian assembly. And remember, we are many times the same. When man was created, he was created in the image of God. And since God's love was his by possession, all these characteristics belonged to him. But when the Fall came, all of it was lost. Once the image of God was marred, love was marred, and man became loveless. Unregenerate man, as well as, a Christian functioning in the flesh, is loveless. So Paul details for us what love is to be. God wants you to know true love, what it is to be blessed. And the real key is simply to learn to love. It is an attitude. A determination to love in spite of circumstances. And this must be a reality for the Christian. God is love, so if God is to be seen in us, it is going to be when we express His Love. We can react to things in the name of love or respond to things in love.

So how does love function and how can it in your life? True love is God shining through us. It is perfect and it is possible, but it must be practiced…It is not easy… And so,

3. Love must be determined…we must want to love (v. 9-13)

*⁹For we know in part, and we prophesy in part, ¹⁰but when completeness comes, what is in part disappears. ¹¹When I was a child, I talked like a child, I thought like a child, I reasoned like a child. When I became a man, I put the ways of childhood behind me. ¹²For now we see only a reflection as in a mirror; then we shall see face to face. Now I know in part; then I shall know fully, even as I am fully known. ¹³And now these three remain: faith, hope and love. But the greatest of these is love.*

True love depends on one person…the giver…You…. Now I realize this is not the world's point of view, and maybe not even yours. But this kind of love emphasizes what you give, not what you get. It's not an emotional workup. It is a decision. We must decide to love!

Love is an attitude. The emphasis is on giving, that is why the King James Version of the Bible uses the word "Charity" for "love" here. The world says do this so people will love you, God says, love in spite of and I will take care of the rest. We cannot understand it completely, but we must trust God. With your love be patient, kind, etc. and God will bless you, not man but God. Love is not dependent on others, but on your relationship to God.

So what is the point anyway? Can we learn to love?...Yes if you know that God is in your life, you can. But one cannot give what they do not have...To love, one needs God.

*My life before becoming a believer in Jesus as my Lord* was one of searching and seeking truth. I was raised in Church, with great people, but only saw Christianity as a religion to act out. I wanted to be my own man, in control of my own life...so I lived a hypocritical life. I "acted" like a Christian. Things went OK in my life until I went to college...and had so much freedom. *I realized I needed Jesus in my life...* in Nov. 1973 as a Sophomore in College. I began listening to friends that were telling me that Life was more than just trying to be a success in this world. After sustaining some injuries in Football, and just being frustrated with life itself, the LORD drew me to a small group of Christians in the Fellowship of Christian Athletes and Baptist Campus Ministries. I saw something in them, I knew I needed it. I also had seen this life in my girlfriend (now my wife) Cheryl, but, I didn't know how to truly become a Believer. Several people began to share with me some truths from God's Word, the Bible. I heard that God Loved me and offered a wonderful plan for my life. I had always heard John 3:16. I mean, I knew God loved me, but I also knew I was a sinner by the way I lived (Cheryl didn't even know). This life had separated from God. Sin was seeking to be Lord of my own life and in control. Sin was disobedience to God. And I was a sinner by nature and by Choice...Romans 3:23 says: "All have sinned and fall short of the

Glory of Glory." That was me for sure. But I was told, Jesus died for my sin. He paid the penalty of death for me (Romans 6:23) says: "but the Wages of sin is death, but the free gift of God is eternal life in Christ Jesus" and Romans 5:8 says: "God demonstrated his love for us in while we were, yet sinners Christ died for us." I was convicted and knew I needed it, and I wanted to be saved. And then I was told that if I would ask Him to forgive me and be willing to repent and turn from my sins He would come into my life and live in me, and I could live forever. (Romans 10:9-10) verified that truth. So by Faith in God's Grace found in Jesus Christ and the Truth found in God's Word, I became a Christian Believer. In literally a closet by myself, I prayed and ask Jesus to save me. I was born again by God's Spirit.

### _You know since I have become a Believer (a Christian)_

I have found Assurance and Security. Jesus changed my life. Knowing that I will spend eternity in heaven when I die gives me peace. Now I want to say quickly, for those who truly know me, I have messed up many, many times over the years even doubting my own salvation, wondering how a true believer can mess up that bad, but God has lovingly drawn me back to Himself, when I repent and return to Him. I am not perfect, but I have been forgiven. I have discovered that Salvation is by God's Grace, Mercy, Love and Forgiveness and not my Works. I am so glad He is the God of a second, third, and twentieth chance. He has saved, forgiven and cleansed me all by His Grace. My family and I are closer, as I get to know Jesus better in that relationship all my relationships are better. My needs have been met over and over again.

I John 5:11-13 says: "those who have the Son of God in their lives have eternal life" So I know that I have eternal and abundant life (full life) because God's Word tells me this Truth. It is such a joy to be a believer in Christ. Jesus Changed my life without a doubt.

I definitely Don't know it all, but He is always there to help me, comfort me, and encourage me. Let Jesus change your life. Get to know God better. The better you know God, the better you can love, for God is love. I am convinced that all marital problems, parenting problems and relationship problems for believers are spiritual problems. The closer one gets to God, the better you can love and eliminate problems. God wants you to! It is so important to share your testimony with your family, so they can understand you. Husband, Wife…What would happen if you loved God's way? I mean *really* learned to love God's way? Parents, Mom, Dad, what would happen if you decided to "love" your children? Grandparents, can you attend this demonstration?

The world is searching for true love, and the only answer is found in a personal relationship with God through His son the Lord Jesus Christ and following His example. Our world is waiting for this example.

*So let's start…Practice makes Perfect, and it is Possible!*

Decide with your will that you will.

Develop the knowledge you need…Jesus!

Determine to make it happen…You can!

Don't make mistakes…Don't let you get in the way.

Love is normal Christian Behavior…*1 John 4: 16 says:*

*And so we know and rely on the love God has for us. God is love. Whoever lives in love lives in God, and God in him.*

So, Do it…Just do it!!!

This is the beginning of doing and being the "Fruit Flavored Family" of faith. You must accept God's Love as your own and ask the LORD to live these out in your life. And you must be obedient to His Word and His Ways. So let's learn how. If you have asked Jesus to be your LORD and Savior, repented of your sins and are wanting Jesus to take control of your life, He will. Right now, just say, "Help me LORD!" *How can one build this characteristic within the family?* Is it possible to see this fruit flourish on our family vine? Sure it is, but how? *Begin with your Personal Quiet time with the Lord.* We can learn what love is from God's Word. He will translate it by the power of His Holy Spirit. It is rational and understandable. Love is not easy or simple, but it is available. Love is also an active power (emotion) that one controls by their own will. Because God lives in your life you can choose to love. So make it an intentional decision to love.(Practice the Principles) It is not always easy to love. Sometimes it takes effort even to those closest to us.. We have found in our 46 years of marriage that each day we must *make the decision to love each other and others.* This love is not something we can attain on our own. It comes from spending time with God each day. Asking God to fill me with His Love, His Spirit, allowing Him to love through me.

One thing Cheryl has done for us to show her love is through notes. Whenever I would have to be out of town I would find love notes throughout my suitcase, in my socks, in my t-shirts, wherever she could find to hide them. She also put notes in our lunchboxes (mine and the children's) as a reminder of her love for us. When our children went on church or school trips we would always send them a note for each day (one of the counselors gave them to them) encouraging them and letting them know we were praying for them. They still have some of those notes. Something I have done for almost 20 years is writing a yearly note and giving it to my family at Christmas. In the letter I reflect on the past year pointing out special times, accomplishments and sharing my love for them. Note writing is free, it doesn't cost a thing and has great rewards! Love is demonstrated in *Words* many times.

Another way we taught our children about love is to love others. God's Word is clear, that we are to love God and love people. There were many mornings when the children would get out of bed and find someone sleeping on the couch. It could be a friend who was having trouble with his wife, a wayward teen, a missionary visiting our community, or even someone with an addiction problem. We wanted to show our children the importance of showing God's love to those in need. We also made it a point to have friends over. We wanted to demonstrate what love and ministry looked like. In order to learn to love it must be demonstrated.

Sharing around the dinner table was another awesome time for our family to share love. It was a way Cheryl, and I could teach what we believe in a relaxed environment. The children felt secure enough in our love for them to share what was on their hearts. We as parents learned much through these discussions. And we would discuss our love for God and them.

After many years of miscommunication Cheryl and I finally hit upon something that worked!! We don't even remember who came up with the ideal, but it has saved us from much distress!

Each week, usually on Monday, since that was my day off, Cheryl and I will spend time going over our weekly calendars. (It could be another day that works better depending on your schedule) We would look at what child had what activity when, where, what my plans were for the week, what Cheryl's were. Once a month we will look at the next couple of months for any big events. We also decided that if we were running late coming home, etc. for more than 15 minutes we would call or text and let the other person know. (This is easy with cell phones now) These two things have been so helpful to us, our marriage, and the life of our family. These times drew us closer together and deepened our love for each other. This set the example of what a marriage focused on love looked like. We were not perfect all the time and when we messed up we would admit it to our children and show them what it looked like to forgive and show Love, like God has shown us in our eternal forgiveness.

Think about what you can do to show some love to your family. Demonstrate it to your children and grandchildren.

Let me close by sharing a few other suggestions.

1. As a grandparent we have enjoyed "Facetime" on our phone and tablets. We make time almost every day to have "breakfast with the grandchildren" During this 15-30 minutes we entertain them while they eat and their parents work around them. We may play puzzles with them or hide and seek or whatever they enjoy. But we always make sure we include an "I love you" or "You are such a blessing to us". Encouragement is a love demonstrator. They know we love them.

2. Send them some just because gifts. We all give great gifts on birthday and holidays, but why not set one or two times a year to send them an inexpensive token of love and tell them so. Tell them you love them so very much and how special they are. Express your love regularly

3. We love to have "grandparent" camp whenever their parents have an opportunity to get away. We seek to make it special for our grandchildren and plan a special time for them. (You need to make sure that you plan and pray) We also started modeling an example of how to do a "quiet time" by having a daily devotion with them. We would sing a simple praise song, read a Bible Story and pray encouraging them to participate. This has been so effective that they even now sometimes will ask for it during our "Facetime" calls. These are awesome times to share stories with them of love and God's Love for them.

4. All of these suggestions can be used at any age or any time in life. After all, Love is from God and as it overflows in our lives, just be natural and follow God's lead. Send them special gifts "just because". Allow them a getaway. Share your love!

5. And don't forget, be creative, pray and ask the LORD to show you how to show LOVE to your family. The internet is full of other suggestions. *Care.com* had list that I found. It included the basics of taking time to listen, posting some of their successes on the "fridge", be supportive, tell them you love them, ask them about their day, give them praise more often, etc.

# Joy

Greek - *Chara*

(cheerfulness, exceeding gladness, and joy)

"Biblical Joy" is a feeling of good pleasure and happiness that is dependent on who Jesus is in our lives. "Genuine Joy" is an attitude of the heart determined by confidence in who God is and what God does. This joy is a result of our intimate relationship with Jesus. "To truly know Christ is to truly know Joy." Rejoicing is expressing that joy.

Psalms 100 says:

*Shout for joy to the LORD, all the earth. Worship the LORD with gladness; come before Him with joyful songs. Know that the LORD is God. It is He who made us, and we are His; we are His people, the sheep of His pasture. Enter His gates with thanksgiving and His courts with praise; give thanks to Him and praise His name.*
*For the LORD is good and His love endures forever; His faithfulness continues through all generations.*

Joy comes from the knowledge of God's Love and Security in our lives. Trust brings joy.

Philippians 4:4 says: *Rejoice in the Lord always. I will say it again: Rejoice!*

Psalms 30:5 says: *For His anger lasts only a moment, but His favor lasts a lifetime; weeping may remain for a night, but rejoicing comes in the morning.*

Psalms 16:11 says: *You have made known to me the path of life; you will fill me with joy in Your presence, with eternal pleasures at Your right hand.*

*JOY...What a wonderful word that enlightens our souls. Joy begins with God and Joy Continues with God, but also, Joy with God is forever.*

Listen to Psalm 16:11:

*You will make known to me the path of life;*
*In Your presence is fullness of joy;*
*In Your right hand there are pleasures forever.*

Joy does not end, because God loves you forever. God promises to make known to us the path of life in order that we may know this joy. For in God's Presence (as we are face to face with God "in Christ Jesus") there is fullness of Joy. There is an overflow of the abundant life of God in us to satisfy the very cravings of the heart. As one writer put it, "Enough, more than enough to satisfy." That is the fullness of God's JOY. And when we have His Joy the results are that God is right there with true happiness and eternal pleasures. When you seek the LORD and His Will and Way daily there is fullness of Joy. And with that Joy God provides true happiness.

The Apostle Paul understood this definition in his writing to the local churches. For example, Joy is a central theme in the book of Philippians. There are many references to some form of either the noun *"joy"* (*chara* in Greek) or the verb *"rejoice"* (*chairo*) in this short letter. Look at a very quick overview:

1. Paul prays for the Philippian believers with joy (*chara*) because of their partnership with him in the gospel. (1:4-5)
2. He rejoices (*chairo*) that his current hardship will turn out for his deliverance, through the prayers of the believers and the help of the Spirit. (1:18-1:19)
3. Paul is convinced that the continuation of his ministry to the Philippians will contribute to their "progress and joy (*chara*) in the faith". (1:25)
4. Paul has joy (*chara*) when the believers are unified and single-minded. (2:2)

48

5.  Paul would rejoice with (*synchairo*) the believers in his sacrifice for the sake of their faith, so that his ministry was not in vain (2:17)
6.  Paul encourages the Philippian believers to have joy (*chairete*) in his life being poured out for them. (2:18)
7.  Paul is eager to send Epaphroditus back to them, so that they can rejoice (*chairo*) in seeing him again and be less anxious about his health. (2:28)
8.  Paul has no problem with frequently repeating the reminder to "rejoice (*chairo*) in the Lord," because he knows how important it is. (3:1)

## *So WHAT can we learn that takes us deeper into God's JOY?*

*1. Don't let circumstances determine your JOY.* Paul's joy was not at all dependent on his circumstances. Although he has been imprisoned for almost four years (1:12-18), he rejoices (1:18). Even if he should be sentenced to death for his ministry, still he would rejoice (2:17, 18). Paul had learned to be content in whatever his present condition (4:11). Paul wanted the Philippians to know bad circumstances do not rob him of joy because his joy is in Christ. Paul's joy was in preaching Jesus Christ and in the fellowship of the followers of Christ. So we also need to declare God as our Source of Joy. We need to believe that He is the Way, the Truth and the LIFE, the Source of JOY. If we simply believe and accept Him as our LORD and Savior or repent and rededicate our life to Him afresh and anew right now, we too can realize this daily joy.

*2. Keep your Mind stayed on Him and receive God's Joy daily as His Gift.* Seek first His Kingdom, His righteousness, His truth, His Word. Spend intimate time with Him *daily.* Listen to Him speak to your heart and obey His directions. Paul's joy was primarily related to Christ. Paul said, "*We . . . glory in Christ Jesus and put no confidence in the*

49

*flesh*" (3:3). That is the explanation of everything else Paul has said. It is Christ that was Paul's joy, confidence and righteousness. When our joy lies in fulfilling our calling, the criticisms and persecutions of the world won't make much difference. Keep your mind on God's Joy as God's Gift to you personally.

*3. Look for God Presence and Pleasures and then Apply them*. In spite of the world's situations and your circumstances, in God's presence there is fullness of JOY! Remember, He's Got YOU! The joy of Paul and the Philippians was related to the bond that joined them (2:17, 18). We don't pay enough attention to that bond these days. There should be great joy in our oneness, our fellowship, our common bond in Christ. Our world seems to seek happiness and joy. What is the difference between joy and happiness? In Philippians, Paul is not talking about happiness in the world when he talks about joy and rejoicing. Happiness is from "hap'…hap is a circumstance, happenstance, happenings, happiness, all the same word group. It has to do with an event, a thing, a happening not a relationship. So the kind of joy that Paul is talking about and calling for, is not the kind of emotional outburst or good feeling that is associated with an event. It is the kind that is associated with a relationship. A daily JOY. It doesn't say, "Rejoice because of what the Lord has given you... It says, "Rejoice in the Lord." Joy (Rejoicing) is the overflow of the relationship with the Lord. The simplest human analogy to it would be the joy of a parent in a newborn baby. It is not the process of childbirth…it's the relationship with the child. That's joy that brings happiness. This kind of joy is not an emotion from a human level, it is produced by the Holy Spirit therefore it is a supernatural emotion. The relationship says my life is in God's hands, my life is in Christ's control, all is well. The hymn writer said, "It is well with my soul," and it is so well with my soul that no matter what is going on around me, I have joy. It's very different from happiness. Why? Because it is the joy in our relationship with Jesus Christ that we enjoy, and it never changes. The LORD is always present. He is ever close. He is ever loving. He is ever securing. He is ever strengthening. He is ever providing. And we trust Him. _Rejoice in the Lord,_ is different than happiness. So Paul Says: Rejoice (Serve …overflow…with a life of joy in the Lord). That is the overflow of the depth of JOY…We can, we do have JOY. We must simply and securely Apply it!

Elizabeth Voyles from the _"organized mom"_ says: "As parents, we wish many things for our children. Things like love, safety, good health, and happiness  and joy. I want my children and grandchildren to have lives full of joy. You might wonder if joy is different than happiness. I think that it is. Happiness is a momentary feeling that may disappear when the moment passes. Often it is dependent on outside factors and influences. Joy comes from something much deeper. It comes from being at peace with who you are and your place in the world. It requires acceptance of your life and what you can and can't control. Joy is finding contentment in your life and the peacefulness that comes with it." Joy is that fruit of the Spirit that comes with realizing that God made you so very special and wants you to be satisfied in His love. He wants the "joy of the LORD to be your strength".

Is it a joy to be a part of your family? In order for this to happen it takes intentional planning-joy just doesn't happen.

_How can one build this characteristic within the family?_ How can the Biblical standard be demonstrated, not lectured into the lives of our family? In the Baldwin household we play games together. This has brought much joy into our lives. Several years in our family history, we have spent time with Cheryl's family at the beach the week after Christmas. One of the traditions was game night where we play various board games. Another was talent show night where each member of the family forms a singing group, or whatever to entertain. This one especially brings joy and much laughter to all. When our grandchildren visit us, we have several games that they always want to play with Poppa and Grandma. Joy is the central element of this time.

There are many other ways to express joy in your family. One night Cheryl placed a beautiful candle by Anna Grace's plate. She explained that Anna Grace had done something special for our neighbor that day. From that time on whenever the candle appeared at the table we knew someone was being honored for some act of kindness that brought "JOY" to someone. That always brought joy to us all! It was our family Joy candle.

Another tradition that has always brought us joy is our family vacations. When the children were small we recognized the importance of getting away together as a family. It didn't have to be anywhere special, but we knew it was vital to our family life. As the children got older they would help us in planning these trips. There are several that stick out in our minds, but any time that is designed to bring joy to your family is a blessing. As we now have grandchildren we have started having a family vacation week. We try our best to make it work for everyone, but know things come up. With the COVID-19 interruption and the years that followed (2020-2021) we have had to adjust plans, but, we are still thinking and planning what else we can do to fill our family with "joy". Remember to pause, pray, and plan. God wants you to know this fruit of Joy in your life. He will help you.

Another trip we planned that had a major effect on our family was the year we were able to go to Africa. Cheryl had been reading a book by Barry St. Clair called _Ignite the Fire: Kindling a Passion for Christ in Your Kids_. In one of the chapters he taught about the need to take your children to a third world country on a mission trip. Our children loved mission trips and so we began praying about this opportunity. There was no way financially we could do this as we were making two house payments at the time having recently moved to a new Church ministry situation. One day the Lord spoke to Cheryl's spirit that if the house sold we could take some of the money and use it for the mission trip. The house had been on the market for several months with no interest. About ten minutes after that thought the phone rang- the realtor was calling to say we had a buyer for the house! We just looked at each other and said, "we're going!" We ended up ministering in South Africa and Malawi, Africa. How all of our eyes were opened! It was during that time God placed on each of our children's heart a deep calling for missions, not necessarily foreign but missions in general. This caused so much "joy" in our hearts as parents. God is so good!

Another memorable vacation was when the children were teenagers. Instead of everyone planning the yearly trip, Garry and I (Cheryl) took charge. We decided to plan something special for each child so with map in hand we began. Each day there was something planned with one specific child in mind. It was a great adventure and lots of fun! They were so excited about anticipating what was coming next. Each one celebrated the other's joy. It was awesome!

Let me close this section with a few final reminders and some more examples for children and grandchildren:

1. *Set the example of Joy in your life. Let them see it.* If you want to teach kids joy then your own life needs to show them what joy looks like. If your life and attitude reflect negativity, stress, and unhappiness it's going to be next to impossible to teach your kids joy. They will have no idea what it looks like. When God blesses, show forth His joy. And even when troubles come, spend time with the LORD so you can demonstrate the joy of trusting in His plan. There are many ways you can bring joy into your families lives- simple everyday routines can be filled with joy. We must keep our eyes

open, ready to see the joy your family can bring!! And. by all means set the example. Have fun, laugh, and just ENJOY!

*2. Don't expect joy, live out the fruit, make it happen.* Vacations during the summer are wonderful. They are opportunities to rest and relax and renew. God wants us to enjoy life to the fullest. Life is really incredible, and we all need to grasp this truth. Jesus said I have come that you may have life and have it more abundantly. The Bible is full of incredible truths. Incredible defined as amazing and wonderful.

The first book that taught people to read in America was the New England Primer. It would use Bible Verses to teach people how to read. It is where we got "Now I lay me down to sleep" etc. It also quotes the opening lines of the Westminster Shorter Catechism to teach basic theology while educating reading. The opening question, in the language of the 17th century, asks, "What is the chief end of man?" The catechist is then to respond, "Man's chief end is to glorify God and enjoy Him forever."

Our Salvation is a life to be enjoyed...God wants that for you! God wants incredible joy in us with Him forever. So How can we learn this truth?

Jesus said in John 15:11 "I have spoken these things to you so that My joy may be in you and your joy may be complete." God wants joy in the midst of all your life and God's joy is incredible. He wants you to know Him and enjoy Him forever. How can we learn God's incredible joy?

Observe the text with me in John 15:11. It begins as we:

1. Learn to Rejoice: "I have spoken these things to you..." When we become a born-again believer we seek after God. We must learn to Rejoice by practicing rejoicing. Rejoicing is a demonstration of Joy. It is delight, a feeling in the heart as a result of God's Grace and Mercy that we proclaim to others. When we sing we rejoice. The delight and the feeling must be expressed. So we Rejoice. We focus on God's Word and His Truth. We Declare the Facts of our Faith. We must stop focusing on the problems in this world. Let's focus on God's goodness. Rejoice! Speak God's truth not just the world's reality of problems and pains.

*Rejoice in the Lord always Paul says, again I say Rejoice.*

We must learn to rejoice, but also we must

2. Learn to Enjoy! the text continues, *"so that My joy may be in you "*. We rejoice so we can enjoy.

Peace, fellowship, and contentment all come from God, and they are already in you. The fruit has grown roots. Rejoicing leads to enjoyment in order that we can learn to enjoy life. We speak God's Truths, so we can realize that Joy is in us.

Rick Warren defined joy in this way: *"Joy is the settled assurance that God is in control of all the details of my life, the quiet confidence that ultimately everything is going to be alright, and the determined choice to Praise God in every situation."*

Rejoice, Enjoy and then you will:

3. Learn to be Joyful! Jesus said, *"I have spoken these things to you that my joy may be in you and your joy may be complete."*

Indeed there is joy in the simple truths of life: vacations, fishing, golf, friendships, resting, drinking coffee, etc. etc. But, to find the incredible, complete Joy that God gives to us as a gift we must keep God in the center of all these areas of. Psalm 16:11 reminds us: *"You reveal the path of life to me; in Your presence is abundant (fullness) of joy; in Your right hand are eternal pleasures."*

God loves you and wants you to know His Joy. But, Joyfulness is when Joy is shared with others. This is our overflow of real joy. Like we do in our Parent/Child or Grandparent/Child relationships when we are together with God in the center. The excitement is evident as we know that God wants us to enjoy Him forever in all things. Peter said it this way in 1 Peter 1: 8: *"You love Him, though you have not seen Him. And though not seeing Him now, you believe in Him and rejoice with inexpressible and glorious (incredible) joy, 9 because you are receiving the goal of your faith, the salvation of your souls."*

Are you ready for Joy in Your Life? Incredible Joy! You can learn how today. Learn to Rejoice. Praise God and speak truth, Sing, share, tell others that your God is Great and greatly to be praised. Rejoice, and give thanks. Learn to Enjoy life! Find this joy in your heart as you focus on God within you. God wants you to enjoy life. Believe His Word of Truth. Learn to be Joyful! Be so full of God's Joy overflowing that others see it in you. Let them see God's fruit all over you. The JOY of the LORD as your strength. Today it is God's gift to you by His Spirit…Incredible Joy.

Take some of the examples given earlier, but especially live out this wonderful fruit of the spirit by planning and living out joy. Joyful habits in the home are a wonderful way to teach kids joy. Sing out loud when you are working. Let joy flow. Make it a point to count your blessings as a family. Teach your children about gratitude. Spending time together as a family is a great way to teach kids joy. Studies have shown that spending money on experiences rather than things makes children happier over the long term. Your entire family will experience more joy from time spent together than from material possessions. And the experiences don't have to be big.

Create small rituals your children and grandchildren can depend on daily or weekly that involve quality family time. Like we shared earlier activities like game nights, movie nights, after dinner walks or drives, and even special family dinners at home or out can all be a part of creating a joyful family life. God's love fills us with joy. In the happy times, in the sad times, in the exciting times, and even in the troubling times we are told in God's Word. The Joy of the Lord is your strength. (Nehemiah 8:10) Learning to choose joy is something that will benefit your children all of their lives. Look around for example to point out the joy in your life. Joy is the root of contentment and peace. It is a choice we make as we are content in all circumstances as God word teaches. And choosing joy helps our children and grandchildren develop compassion, empathy, and kindness. This fruit of joy bubbles over in our fruits of the Spirit. Jesus reminded us in John 15 that He wanted our "joy" to be full. Of all the things we could use more of in the world, joy is one of them. But it doesn't always come naturally. It is in a believers life but must be expressed in obedience to be evident. My prayer is that you will "choose" to use these ideas to teach your children and grandchildren joy and you all benefit from a life filled with the contentment that joy brings to your family.

# Peace

Greek - *Eirene (Irenay)*...
(Peace and quiet...Rest)

Sharing the fruit of peace with your family is a blessing for all. Peace is freedom from fears and conflicts. It is the security of the LORD and our family.

2 Peter 3:14 says: *So then, dear friends, since you are looking forward to this, make every effort to be found spotless, blameless and at peace with Him.*

Peace is a move toward reconciliation, especially with relationships within the family. Peace is a truly wonderful way to find a home as a refuge from the storms of life. Peace is awesome. God wants us to know this peace. God's Word speaks volumes about peace. For example: In Romans 12:18 tells us: *If it is possible, as far as it depends on you, live at peace with everyone.*

Matthew 5:9 says: *Blessed are the peacemakers, for they will be called sons of God.*

Proverbs 16:7 says: *When a man's ways are pleasing to the LORD, He makes even his enemies live at peace with him.*

Philippians 4:6-7 says: *Do not be anxious about anything, but in everything, by prayer and petition, with thanksgiving, present your requests to God. And the peace of God, which transcends all understanding, will guard your hearts and your minds in Christ Jesus.*

Psalms 29:11 says: *The LORD gives strength to His people; the LORD blesses His people with peace.*

John 14:27 says; *Peace I leave with you; My peace I give you. I do not give to you as the world gives. Do not let your hearts be troubled and do not be afraid.*

So with all the negative words in our world, how can we be positive and speak words and live lives of peace?

…Is there anything positive we can say and do???

A mother cat lived under the porch of a country house with her kittens. One day a dog came toward the porch. The Mother cat jumped out and barked loudly…Woof, Woof, Woof…. The dog ran scared…The mother went back and said, "that children is just one of the values of learning a second language…."

With all the negative language in our world, how can we learn the positive words of life? For all the dogs threatening our homes what can we say to instill hope and peace?

There are some Positive Principals for Living in God's Word. One of my favorites is found in Proverbs 3:1-6:

*My son, do not forget My teaching, but keep My commands in your heart, for they will prolong your life many years and bring you prosperity. Let love and faithfulness never leave you; bind them around your neck, write them on the tablet of your heart. Then you will win favor and a good name in the sight of God and man. Trust in the LORD with all your heart and lean not on your own understanding; in all your ways acknowledge Him, and He will make your paths straight.*

Probably the greatest need and desire in the life of a family is peace and security. It is the refuge of life. Knowing this peace, sets the tone of family acceptance, confidence and assurance. It reminds us to remind ourselves of God's love, peace and faithfulness. This is where real assurance proceeds from. It is a promise of God. The Psalmist made it clear in Psalms 62:5-12 when he said:

*Find rest, O my soul, in God alone; my hope comes from Him. He alone is my rock and my salvation; He is my fortress; I will not be shaken. My salvation and my honor depend on God; He is my mighty rock, my refuge. Trust in Him at all times, O people; pour out your hearts to Him, the highborn are but a lie; if weighed on a balance, they are nothing; together they are only a breath. Do not trust in extortion or take pride in stolen goods; though your riches increase, do not set your heart on them. One thing God has spoken, two things have I heard: that You, O God, are strong, and that you, O Lord, are loving. Surely You will reward each person according to what he has done.*

**We can have high hopes in our God...
because of His Peace, Love and Faithfulness.**

So in even our world today we can have hope and peace because God says so...<u>In John 14...</u> Jesus reminded His disciples. *<u>Do not let your hearts be troubled...Trust in God.</u>* He is talking about God's sovereignty and power. In the New Testament, this high hope was fulfilled in the Lord Jesus Christ. In our lives now, our high hopes and peace are built on nothing less than Jesus, his blood and righteousness.

We are not immune as believers from the heartaches of the world. Jesus reminds us in <u>Matthew 5:43-45</u>

*You have heard that it was said, 'Love your neighbor and hate your enemy.' But I tell you: Love your enemies and pray for those who persecute you, that you may be sons of your Father in heaven. He causes His sun to rise on the evil and the good and sends rain on the righteous and the unrighteous.*

We live in a fallen creation...full of headaches and heartaches, so what is a believer to do? Remember when heartaches come, we, through our trust in the Lord our God, can deal with and work through them. We can turn our hopes and heartaches into actual Hallelujahs. Hallelujah means *Praise the Lord*. It is a natural overflow of a believer. How can we be positive in a negative world? Hold on to the Promises of God…Trust in the Lord

In John 14:27…Jesus said, *My peace I give you..* Always remember, God is the one who is in control. Tell yourself, God Loves me best, loves me most, God loves me as my Father; therefore, I can rest in His power. God is in control. We can always rest in the peace of God.

The prophet Isaiah said in … Isaiah 32:17:

*The fruit of righteousness will be peace; the effect of righteousness will be quietness and confidence forever.*

Today are you looking for peace…positive truth in a negative world….It is only a prayer away…Bow your heads, and pray with me:

*Lord, I have done things my way long enough!*

*Forgive me for only looking through my eyes, I want to look with Spiritual eyes at your Promises God. Help me to learn to trust, Getting to know You better Lord and Resting there in Your Power. Teach me the truths of trust and confidence… That I may find Your Peace!*

### Now…How can one build peace within the family?

To build peace in the family, one must begin with some Basic Rules in the family. These are for everyone, but especially during the child-rearing years.

### No Dis-obedience and No Dis-honesty

These were two basic rules in the Baldwin household. The children knew that if they disobeyed directly, or were dishonest (lied intentionally), that would warrant a lovingly administered spanking. As we told them you made the choice to have this spanking. It is so important that everyone knows and follows through with the guidelines. Later, as the children grew we added No Dis-Respect to the Basic rules. This didn't deserve a spanking, but time outs were common as they began to understand respect. Building peace in your family involves communication-everyone must be on the same team- success requires teamwork. Peace requires obedience, honesty and respect. This teamwork begins during the preschool years-from the very beginning-each member needs to know they are important to the family. Feeling a vital part of the family will make the tough time easier if everyone is secure in their position. They have peace built into their lives. We heard of one family that was having trouble with consistent discipline with their children. It was causing major problems in their family. The parents decided to sit down with each other when all was going well. They took 3x5 cards and wrote down any situation they could think of that would warrant discipline. On the back they decided and wrote out the plan of action. They then went over these cards with the children so they would know what to expect. Whenever a situation arose mom or dad would just go to their box of cards and proceed from there. It took away much stress and frustration. Everyone knew what to expect. What a great idea! Of course the cards would need to be revised, as the children got older. It also eased the tension for the parents when they were in the "heat of the moment." We applied this plan in our family, and it worked. To ensure peace there must be a plan, until maturity is reached. Again, let me emphasis all this plan is revealed and renewed with your daily time alone with God. This time is so vitally important because of how God speaks to you to give you more plans and ideas.

### Opportunities to grow

When the children were younger there would be days when I arrived home and could tell Cheryl had had a busy or stressful day. On my own I wanted nothing more to do than to sit down and relax. After all, I had worked hard all day- I deserved a break. (And Cheryl hadn't...LOL) Sensing Cheryl's frustration and cold shoulder we came up with a game plan. We called it "Cheryl's Chill Time". Each night when I came in I would ask her if she needed her "chill time", if so I would take over and she could do whatever for the next 30 minutes or so. In turn if I had had a stressful day she would give me the same privilege. This simple plan made for much peace in our household. We were seeking to be a giver of peace for each other.

Another issue we need to discuss in talking about peace is anger. Everyone get angry. The important thing we need to learn and teach is how to handle our anger. There are many wrong ways to express our anger- yelling, throwing things, slamming doors, hitting, keeping it inside, and not talking, to name a few. How do you handle anger? How do your children handle anger? Do you ever see yourself in them when they are angry? One of the main goals in our family was teaching our children how to handle their anger. Our oldest, Jeremiah, truly knew how to "push" Caleb's buttons. He knew exactly what to do or say to upset Caleb. This was an area we really had to work on. It was not fun to see our youngest so out of control- he didn't enjoy it either. We had to come up with a game plan, something that would teach our children how to be at peace with each other. We taught them how to listen to each other, treat each other with respect, and how to fight fairly. We realized that first they had to see how we handled our anger with each other, we as parents had to set the standard. This didn't and doesn't happen overnight. It takes time and patience- and lots of work. Now, let's close this fruit of peace with a few game plans to work on with your children and grandchildren.

Again on the internet there are dozens of wonderful websites, some Christian based and some not, but all can give you a few ideas to spark your creativity in teaching Peace as a fruit of the Spirit. For example at yes.com we find a few suggestions: Outer peace begins with inner peace. Teach your children and grandchildren how to have a "quiet time" and find the peace of the LORD. Show them by example of what that looks like. "Children and adults need special places that give them a sense of privacy and peace, and that can serve as a quiet refuge for times when hurt or angry feelings might lead to violent words or actions. It could be a room or just a corner, where any family member can go for quiet reflection or to work through turbulent feelings." If someone goes to that spot, make sure they know they are safe to take a time out, a quiet time to find God's Peace. Find peace in nature. Turn off the television and the computer and go outside. Take your children or grandchildren for a walk or let them explore nature with you. Talk to them about the beauty of nature and how God allows His creation to comfort our souls with His peace. Engage your children's and your grandchildren's heads, hands and hearts. Young children need a direct, hands-on experience of giving. They love to make things, small and large—their own cards, tree ornaments, cookies, or bread—for neighbors, family, or friends. Think of things they can do that generate peace in their lives. Make it a family tradition during Thanksgiving or Christmas. Establish a "family foundation." I love this idea, and wish I would have thought of it. (for more information check out "alliance for children" This thought is from a 2013 article.) To develop a "family foundation" create a homemade bank for donations—a miniature family foundation. Parents, children, visitors, and friends can put money in the bank. Children can be introduced to tithing when they receive gifts, earnings, or allowance. Then choose a charity together —one that has personal meaning for the children especially—to give to. As the children mature, talk to them more about the needs of the world and ways to help." Every year, we have given gifts in our children's honor. For example a local "Coats for kids" drive inspired us to give a coat in each of our grandchildren's size. We gave our grandchildren a certificate that we have given a coat in their name. Remember we are living in a world that seems to know no peace at times. Your children and grandchildren are talking about it. Don't be so over opinionated that they do not feel comfortable talking to you about how they feel and why. Create ways to keep the discussions real and let them know peace by talking about peace. Encourage your older children and grandchildren to study a conflict-ridden area of the world, looking at it from two or more perspectives. They'll learn that every conflict has many layers and that to build peace one must work respectfully with all sides. And don't' forget to "face local needs. Help children become comfortable with the people in your community who need help—the elderly, the disabled, the poor."

Well, you've read quite a bit so far. What about a homework assignment? Are you ready? As a result of reading this material take some time together and ask: What can I do to make these principals work in my home? Discuss this with your spouse.

# Patience

Greek – *Makrothomia*
(patient longsuffering, endurance)

Many people do not even like the word patience because they feel it means suffering in order to learn a lesson. But, for the fruit flavored family patience is maturity. It is learning to wait on the Lord. It is God helping you in the midst of your family issues. The Word of God is full of wisdom when it comes to understanding patience.

Isaiah 30:18…says: *"Yet the LORD longs to be gracious to you; He rises to show you compassion. For the LORD is a God of justice. Blessed are all who wait for Him!"*

Isaiah 40:28-31…says: *Do you not know? Have you not heard? The LORD is the everlasting God, the Creator of the ends of the earth. He will not grow tired or weary, and His understanding no one can fathom. He gives strength to the weary and increases the power of the weak. Even youths grow tired and weary, and young men stumble and fall; but those who hope in the LORD will renew their strength. They will soar on wings like eagles; they will run and not grow weary, they will walk and not be faint.*

Psalms 27:14…says: *Wait for the LORD; be strong and take heart and wait for the LORD.*

Proverbs 16:32…says: *Better a patient man than a warrior, a man who controls his temper than one who takes a city.*

Romans 5:3-4…says: *Not only so, but we also rejoice in our sufferings, because we know that suffering produces perseverance; perseverance, character; and character, hope.*

So what do you sense as you read these Scriptures? There are dozens of others, but just to get us started, we want to focus on patience as the Fruit of the Spirit that God displays in our life when we reach out to Him in times of stress, anger, and frustration. God is saying "wait" on me and I will take care of all things. We are called to be apprentices of Jesus in kingdom living, and this requires time, development, and patience.

Growth in this area of patience is never automatic or easy. Progress in following Jesus necessitates an intentional and ongoing commitment to a specific course of spiritual formation. Our daily goal is to place ourselves under the conditions favorable to growth and look to God for our spiritual formation. He uses different paces and methods with each person. Our own growth and maturity may be different for our children and grandchildren. As nature teaches us, growth is not exactly the same—like a vine or a tree, there may be more growth in a single month than in all the rest of the year. If we fail to accept this uneven developmental process, we will be impatient with God and with ourselves as we wait for the next growth spurt or special infusion of grace. We must "wait" for the LORD. That is the key to maturity and application of this fruit.

In a culture that promotes instant gratification, the "right now" mentality, it can be tiring for us to wait patiently for God's timing. But the fact is that we are as incapable of changing ourselves through our own efforts as we are of trying to help God transform us more quickly.

By His grace, through His grace, and in His grace, the Lord invites us to cooperate with the formative work of His Holy Spirit in our lives by engaging in the disciplines of faith, repentance, and obedience and by trusting in His ways and in His timing. Inevitably, God's timing will seem painfully slow to us, but as we grow in wisdom, we learn to be more patient with the divine process, knowing that He alone knows what we need and when we need it. Thus, spiritual formation is nourished by years of disciplined dedication and obedience to the sovereign call of God to each of us. Indeed, we will fail and disobey and do many foolish things throughout the process, but the application of the Spiritual Fruit of Patience means that we get up and return to Jesus each time we fall.

How can one build Patience within the family?

Look for opportunities to teach patience by example. Take a good look at yourself and your life and teach by example.

In 1982, I was working Grove Park Baptist church *in Burlington, North Carolina* and was serving as a youth minister. We were in the middle of a building project, and it was my job to check the doors in the building before I left each day. I would take a flashlight, since the power was not on yet, and go through the building to see if any persons happened to still be in the building. Sometimes, we would find the homeless or transients hiding in the rooms in order to spend the night there. One evening I noticed that a door was open in the bathroom. As I looked in I noticed my flashlight seemed to reflect off of a person standing over in the corner. As I began to address this issue, wouldn't you know it, my flashlight went out and would not work. There I stood in the dark. And so I shook the flashlight and only occasionally did it work. I was terrified, but I didn't want the man to know it. So, I shouted to the man in the corner that he had to leave, but he did not respond. Again the light continued to flicker on and off and all I could see what this figure in the corner not moving. So I took one step toward him and as the light flashed on, I noticed he took a step toward me. I tried to talk in a stern voice again, and said, "You need to come out of here" and as the light flashed on again, I saw him looking right at me. He was ugly looking and big. But I continued toward him determined to get him out of there.

I took one more step toward him and then we got face-to-face as the light came back on brightly, *and there I stood looking into a mirror.*

We all need to take a good look at ourselves, don't we? We have many examples in our lives that we can use to teach and train our children and grandchildren in the area of patience.

How much time do you spend in the car with your children and grandchildren? How do they see you behave in the car? Do you yell at other drivers, blow your horn unnecessarily, mutter under your breath? What kind of example of patience do you set for your children and grandchildren?

Do you wait before making a purchase or do you buy on impulse? Use everyday situations to teach your children and grandchildren patience. We live in such a "I gotta have it now" world where patience is not valued. As parents we need to be intentional in teaching this fruit of the Spirit. You could do a Bible study on patience. Also, real life circumstances and situations are great teaching tools. Earlier in the book we told you about our trip to Africa and how the money was provided. We had been frustrated that our home in Burlington had not sold in almost 2 years. It was during that time we all had to trust and wait on the Lord. This is patience applied. Our children learned they didn't always get what they wanted when they wanted it. It was a great time to teach patience. In the end we saw the "why" of our wait. Not only did we get to go on that life-changing trip we also made enough money on the sale of the house to put into college savings.

So let's review a few additional suggestions:

Cheryl has always told me that the attention span of a child is usually equal to their age. A one-year-old gives you one minute, a two-year-old two minutes and so forth. So remember when your child is young, it's hard for them to grasp the need for or benefits of patience. Not only is their concept of time not quite developed, but neither is their sense of delayed gratification. They want it now!

So when you set a timeframe for something (for example, when they will get the snack you promised them or when you'll arrive at your destination, etc.),  they're going to ask if it's time yet…frequently. We have all heard it. So teach patience by staying patient. Respond to their question, do not react to it, even if they have asked a dozen times. Remember, they're not trying to be selfish or mean spirited in their questions—they simply don't have the capability to apply this fruit of the spirit yet. It is your job to demonstrate it for them. Yelling at your child or otherwise punishing them for asking too many times will reinforce the idea that waiting is a negative experience. However, staying calm and positive while they wait reinforces that waiting can be a positive experience. Remember we are teaching patience.

I know this next suggestion is not going to be well received either, but researchers tell us that the use of a iPad, phone, tablet or a video game is not teaching them the fruit of patience because you are not interactive with them. If we are going to invest in developing the "fruits of the Spirit" in the lives of our children and grandchildren, we must be present. We must be in the moment with them. This is so hard I know, but God will bless as we do. Find some different ways to help the time pass in a more productive, engaging way. Allow your child to feel time passing while still having a positive experience through it. We have played the alphabet game in the car where we search for the letters of the alphabet in signs around us…For example A…Arbys,  B…Bojangles, C…Closed Road, etc. etc.

Be accurate in your time and gift promises. When you say we will be there in a few minutes that is tough to understand. Be accurate and then be creative in teaching them how to "wait". Remember you are nurturing the fruit of patience.

And finally make sure you share information with your children and grandchildren. Give them age-appropriate information, in order to keep them involved. One such example would be: "Christmas is 12 sleeps away." Or "The theme park is about one movie long away."

Remember, the LORD continues to be so patient with us, let's make sure we share and live this truth with our family.

# Kindness

Greek-*Chestotes*

## (kindness, usefulness)

One of the most well accepted character traits of our society is kindness. It is one word that almost everyone understands or wants to understand. But, for the fruit flavored family kindness is an overflow.

Kindness is defined here as compassion, which is recognizing needs and helping with care and respect. It is the natural character of a Christian.

Proverbs 3:3 says: *"Let love and faithfulness never leave you; bind them around your neck, write them on the tablet of your heart."*

James 2:14-17 says: *"What good is it, my brothers, if a man claims to have faith but has no deeds? Can such faith save him? Suppose a brother or sister is without clothes and daily food. If one of you says to him, "Go, I wish you well; keep warm and well fed," but does nothing about his physical needs, what good is it? In the same way, faith by itself, if it is not accompanied by action, is dead."*

1 Peter 3:8-9 says: *"Finally, all of you, live in harmony with one another; be sympathetic, love as brothers, be compassionate and humble. Do not repay evil with evil or insult with insult, but with blessing, because to this you were called so that you may inherit a blessing."*

### How can one build kindness into a life?

Once again kindness is something our children learn from us. It is something that is caught. As we walk in obedience to God's Spirit leading us, it is own natural overflow of faith. Even preschoolers can learn kindness. They can draw pictures for a sick neighbor;

help you bake bread or cookies for a friend. While on vacation we would do random acts of kindness, but we called them "intentional acts of kindness". They were something that we planned to do on purpose. For instance we were at a restaurant in Colorado and talking with the waitress. From our conversation we learned she was a single mom struggling to make ends meet. Upon recommendation of our oldest, Jeremiah, we decided to leave her a tip with a note telling her we wanted her to use it to take her children out for something special. Keep your eyes open, God will provide many opportunities for you to mirror kindness to your children.

Another way to show and teach kindness is by our friendships. Do you remember as a child Fridays at school meant Show and Tell Day? I remember searching the house on Thursday nights for some treasure to take and then getting up in front of the class on Friday and telling them about it. That is what God calls us to do. Show our friends love and kindness and tell them about His Love. It is God's love in action.

### *So what really does it mean to be a kind friend?*

What is Friendship anyway? Friendship is *kindness expressed* to others. In a survey of 40,000 by Barna research, people said that the top 3 qualities of a friend are…1. Can be trusted  2. Loyal 3. Cares about me…

Now I think we are getting closer to what a friend is and how kindness is recognized in one's life. C.S. Lewis said… "Friendship is born at that moment when one person says to another, "What… you too, I thought I was the only one?"

So let's go a step further in defining and showing the reality of Friendship so let's see what it says. Let's look in the Bible where one can find the true meaning of genuine friendship. In John's

Gospel chapter 15, Jesus got His students (disciples) together to teach them what real friendship consists of and in doing so teaches kindness in action...Basically He taught that:

1.  Friendship requires Commitment (John 15: 12-14)

God's love for us was so great that He gave His life for us. Casual Friendship cost nothing. Real, Serious Friendship costs everything. It takes time, effort, and patience. Kindness must be practiced. We must not ever take friendship for granted. Jesus sets that example and asks us to do the same, as He goes on to say, "We are His Friends if we love one another." In other words, we show God we love Him when we love people. 1 John 4:11-21 says it so clearly:

*"Dear friends , since God so loved us, we also ought to love one another. No one has ever seen God; but if we love one another, God lives in us, and His love is made complete in us. We know that we live in Him and He in us, because He has given us His Spirit. God is love. Whoever lives in love lives in God, and God in Him. In this way, love is made complete among us. We love each other because he first loved us. If anyone says, "I love God," yet hates his brother, he is a liar. For anyone who does not love his brother, whom he has seen, cannot love God, whom he has not seen. And he has given us this command: Whoever loves God must also love his brother.*

Friendship requires commitment to love like God...but How?

2. Friendship is a Gift from God (v. 15)

The fruit of the Spirit, kindness, is the overflow of the Lord in our lives resulting in friendship. What is so great about being a believer is that God even teaches me how to be a good friend. It is a part of my nature as a believer in the Lord Jesus Christ. It is in me as a gift from God. I am called by God and taught by God to be a friend and to demonstrate kindness. Now again, What does that mean?…Kind, loyal, trusting, and caring. Everyone wants a friend, and anyone can be a friend.

The 23rd Psalm is a great example of God's gift of Friendship and how God loves and takes care of us like a Shepherd does His Sheep. Friendship requires commitment. it is God's gift.

3. Friendship is a Command from God (v. 16-17)

But…it is our Choice… I not only want to be your friend, but God also commands me too. It is a part of my calling as a believer. But…I must choose to obey and be a Friend!

It is why we exist as the Church…To love God and to love people. We are called and commanded to be Kind.

Let me illustrate. I remember growing up, playing playground games, and it came time to be "chosen" to be on a team. There you stand, hoping to be chosen and wanted. I remember my best friend not choosing me, and I said to him, "you are not my friend anymore." I went home so mad and sad. But you know, I was the one with a choice. He didn't act like a friend, but I still could forgive him and give him another chance. Friendship really is a choice isn't it? You decide and I decide. Do you remember the notes you may have gotten when you were younger?

*Can I be your Friend? (Check one)*

*Yes No*

The greatest gift you can give someone is the gift of an invitation: an invitation to be a Friend and an invitation to a relationship with God.

The greatest gift anyone could ever get is a personal relationship with God, forgiveness for their sin and a place in heaven forever. If you have not accepted Christ personally into your life, we want to invite you to do so in just a moment. This may seem like a strange part of the book to invite you to Christ and His Salvation, but believe us, no place or time is too strange. God wants you to be His friend for eternity and we do to.

True friends want to see us continue to grow. The writer of Proverbs has said that friends help to sharpen us, to become sharp spiritually takes a little bit at a time. He compares this type of friendship to iron that is sharpened by iron. Think of a blacksmith who makes swords. He takes a hammer and takes out a piece of iron and works on it slowly and continuously until it takes the shape and sharpness of a sword. Friends are always challenging us and even pushing us to be all that God wants for us to be. You may be saying to yourself, "I wish I had a friend like that!" The second half of Proverbs 18:24 which we read earlier says

*"... But there is a friend who sticks closer than a brother."* So one more time, let us invite you to let Jesus be your Best Friend. There are some very important reasons to do so. First, Jesus deserves to be your Best Friend because He already knows you better than anyone else. One more definition of a friend is someone who knows all about us and likes us anyway. Well, no one better fulfills that qualification as Jesus.

Secondly, Jesus deserves to be your Best Friend because He had done more for you than anyone else. John 15:13 says:

*"Greater love has no one than this,*
*than to lay down one's life for his friends."*

And finally, Jesus deserves to be your Best Friend because He will always be there when you need Him. The words of the hymn, "What A Friend We Have In Jesus" says it well:

*"What A Friend We Have In Jesus,*
*All Our Sins And Griefs To Bear*
*What A Privilege To Carry*
*Everything To God In Prayer*

*Oh, What Peace We Often Forfeit,*
*Oh, What Needless Pain We Bear,*
*All Because We Do Not Carry*
*Everything To God In Prayer."*

Earlier, we said we would give you an opportunity to receive Jesus as your Best Friend. Those of you who cannot honestly say today that you have experienced a relationship with Jesus Christ we want to extend an invitation for you to do so today. Cheryl and I want to introduce you to someone who will be the greatest friend you have ever had. He is a friend who has already accepted you just as you are. He is a friend who has already paid your sin debt on the cross. He is a friend who is always accessible and who will never leave you. If you would like to accept him as your friend and your Savior we want to lead you in a prayer that will allow you to establish that friendship. This prayer is not a magic formula, which must be repeated in just the right order but is just a guide for you to make your own prayer to the Lord.

*" Lord Jesus, I want to be your friend and I am thankful that You want to be mine. I realize that I have sinned, and that sin has separated me from You. I recognize that friendship would not be possible without the fact that You have already paid for my sin on the cross. I want to accept what You have personally done for me. Lord, please come into my life, forgive me of my sin, and be the LORD and Savior of my life."*

Now if you prayed that prayer for the first time and you really meant business then welcome to the family of God. Please email us at pastorgarry@gmail.com and tell us of your decision so we can send you some additional material to help you grow. God bless you in your new "friendship" with your Lord and Savior, Jesus Christ.

# Goodness

Greek - *Agothosone*
(goodness, moral completeness)

I can remember growing up and my mother always saying as she sent me off to school, church, or to a friend's house: "Now, be good!" For the believer goodness is defined by a common, yet complex term, **Integrity**. Integrity meaning doing what is right with the right motives, right thinking, and right action. It is honorable, trustworthy, moral completeness. It is not what you understood when your mother said to be good. It is a fruit of God's Spirit.

Proverbs 20:7 says... *a righteous man leads a blameless life; ("a life of integrity") blessed are his children after him.*

### This is Simple Integrity...

Years ago we were teaching our children about integrity and that goodness was doing what was right all time. It was raining one day as we finished our shopping at Wal-Mart. Cheryl and the children had run to the car and I was taking the shopping cart out to the car with our things. The bin to return the carts was on the other side of the lot and as I finished unloading, I noticed several carts gathered on the parking lot island next to our car. Knowing the "right thing" to do was easy, but it took integrity to make the long trip in the rain to return the cart to the right place. It was worth it all when I came back to the car soaking wet and my oldest son said: "You passed the test daddy", You were a "Man of Integrity". Wow! What I had preached the week before after a men's conference on Integrity was heard and understood by my children. They were watching me.

### Who will you be when no one is looking?

This is a question we all have to answer, isn't it not? It is the question of Integrity. It is the definition of goodness. Integrity…is doing what is right at all times. Webster defines it as "firm moral values". Doing the right thing. Again, it is what mother meant when she said, "Be Good".

Integrity in its root form is Integer… a whole number…Being complete. It is found throughout the Word of God. The lifestyle of Integrity is urged.

In Deuteronomy 6:18-19 it says: *Do what is right and good in the LORD's sight, so that it may go well with you, and you may go in and take over the good land that the LORD promised on oath to your forefathers, thrusting out all your enemies before you, as the LORD said.*

2 Thessalonians 3:13 says: *And as for you, brothers, never tire of doing what is right.*

Romans 12:17 says: *Do not repay anyone evil for evil. Be careful to do what is right in the eyes of everybody.*

Psalms 106:3 says: *Blessed are they who maintain justice, who constantly do what is right.*

2 Corinthians 8:21 says: *For we are taking pains to do what is right, not only in the eyes of the Lord but also in the eyes of men.*

### Integrity is an important part of being a believer.

It means Moral Excellence. It is a virtue, using God's Standards to live by. It is obeying God's directions. So How does one do that?

We have an epidemic of low self-esteem in our world. So many try to fit them with world standards. Really, low self-esteem is not a bad thing if you understand it and don't stay there God wants to use all of us for His Glory…So how do we use God's standards to live by?

<u>*Moral Excellence begins with Character (1 Corinthians 1:27-28)*</u>

*27 But God chose the foolish things of the world to shame the wise; God chose the weak things of the world to shame the strong. 28 He chose the lowly things of this world and the despised things-and the things that are not-to nullify the things that are,*

Moral Excellence is lived out behavior…How?

1. Know your Identity (Who we are) Child of God.

John 1:12 *'But to all who did receive Him, who believed in his name, He gave the right to become children of God,'*

Galatians 3:26 *"for in Christ Jesus you are all sons of God, through faith."*

2. Destiny (What God plans for us to be "in Christ")

Ephesians 1:18-23 *"I pray also that the eyes of your heart may be enlightened in order that you may know the hope to which He has called you, the riches of His glorious inheritance in the saints, 19 and His incomparably great power for us who believe. That power is like the working of His mighty strength, 20 which He exerted in Christ when He raised him from the dead and seated Him at His right hand in the heavenly realms, 21 far above all rule and authority, power and dominion, and every title that can be given, not only in the present age but also in the one to come. 22 And God placed all things under His feet and appointed Him to be head over everything for the church, 23 which is His body, the fullness of Him who fills everything in every way."*

Ephesians 3:18-21 *"may have power, together with all the saints, to grasp how wide and long and high and deep is the love of Christ, 19 and to know this love that surpasses knowledge-that you may be filled to the measure of all the fullness of God. 20 Now to Him who is able to do immeasurably more than all we ask or imagine, according to His power that is at work within us, 21 to Him be glory in the church and in Christ Jesus throughout all generations, for ever and ever! Amen."*

## 3. Integrity (obedience to God's promptings)

John 14:15 *"If you love Me, you will keep My commandments. 16 And I will ask the Father, and He will give you another Helper, to be with you forever, 17 even the Spirit of truth, whom the world cannot receive, because it neither sees Him nor knows Him. You know Him, for He dwells with you and will be in you.*

Col 1:27 *To them God chose to make known how great among the Gentiles are the riches of the glory of this mystery, which is Christ in you, the hope of glory. 28 Him we proclaim, warning everyone and teaching everyone with all wisdom, that we may present everyone mature in Christ. 29 For this I toil, struggling with all His energy that he powerfully works within me.*

## 4. Availability (Willing to hear and respond)

John 14:12 *"Truly, truly, I say to you, whoever believes in Me will also do the works that I do; and greater works than these will he do, because I am going to the Father. 13 Whatever you ask in My name, this I will do, that the Father may be glorified in the Son. 14 If you ask Me anything in My name, I will do it.*

1 Corinthians 2:9 However, as it is written: *"No eye has seen, no ear has heard, no mind has conceived what God has prepared for those who love Him"*-

And so when we understand and live it out, what does it look like? How can we know what the qualities or fruit looks like? Let me share 8….Qualities of Goodness (that is Integrity and Moral Excellence lived out)

1. Obedience (Doing what God says to do) God wants us to obey Him. This begins with our attitude. It is a decision and shows our respect and integrity to ourselves and others. (Luke 6:46) *"Why do you call me, 'Lord, Lord,' and do not do what I say?*

1 John 5:3 *This is love for God: to obey his commands. And his commands are not burdensome,*

2. Holiness (Holiness is obedience lived out) (Isaiah 35:8) When the natural evidence of obedience is displayed without even "thinking" it is what Holiness looks like.

And a highway will be there; it will be called the Way of Holiness. The unclean will not journey on it; it will be for those who walk in that Way; wicked fools will not go about on it.

3. Pure Heart (Honest Confession of Self and Sin) It is important to keep sin and self where it cannot hide and keep you in bondage with dishonesty. A pure heart seeks to be open and honest. (Psalms 24:4) He who has clean hands and a pure heart, who does not lift up his soul to an idol or swear by what is false.

4. Contrite Heart (Repentant Life) This is the constant seeking to do the right thing in every situation and circumstance. (Psalms 34:14) Turn from evil and do good; seek peace and pursue it.

5. Fear of God (Respect and Humility toward God) When we understand and decide to honor God and His Word in all things and at all times. (Deuteronomy 10:12)And now, O Israel, what does the LORD your God ask of you but to fear the LORD your God, to walk in all his ways, to love him, to

serve the LORD your God with all your heart and with all your soul,

6. Faithfulness (Consistent Obedience) This is both a decision and dedication to do what one knows is right at all times. (Revelation 2:10) Do not be afraid of what you are about to suffer. I tell you; the devil will put some of you in prison to test you, and you will suffer persecution for ten days. Be faithful, even to the point of death, and I will give you the crown of life.

_Luke 16:10_ *"Whoever can be trusted with very little can also be trusted with much, and whoever is dishonest with very little will also be dishonest with much.*

7. Seeks and Loves God (Consistent Q.T. and Compassionate Lifestyle) Again, this is the practice of our faith by "doing" what we know is best each and every day. Living a daily, devoted, faith walk. (Deuteronomy 4:29) But if from there you seek the LORD your God, you will find him if you look for him with all your heart and with all your soul. (1 John 4:19-21) We love because he first loved us. 20 If anyone says, "I love God," yet hates his brother, he is a liar. For anyone who does not love his brother, whom he has seen, cannot love God, whom he has not seen. 21 And he has given us this command: Whoever loves God must also love his brother.

8. Servant of the Lord (Helping others…small things, doing what is right) Jesus always taught the importance of being a "servant" and the greatness of living this out. It is simple truth lived out. (Colossians 3:23-24) Whatever you do, work at it with all your heart, as working for the Lord, not for men, 24 since you know that you will receive an inheritance from the Lord as a reward. It is the Lord Christ you are serving.

*Moral Excellence is God's Goodness lived out in me! Listening to God's Word and Obeying His Promptings.*

The world will do this and that and say it is right, but, what about you? The message for the *Fruit Flavored Family* today is clear. We must visit and revisit integrity on a daily basis. Simply doing what is right is the way to teach integrity, moral excellence (goodness). It truly is a personal decision. What will be your decision? So the real question is, How can you maintain Integrity? As a parent, a child, or anyone in the family how can we?

1. Begins with Assurance of Salvation- (Assured)  Integrity comes from your relationship with God.

John 15 says: *"I am the vine; you are the branches. If a man remains in me and I in him, he will bear much fruit; apart from me you can do nothing.*

No pretending...no joking...Check out your relationship with God. Are you assured that you are saved?

2. It continues with Seeking the truth... (Active Faith)

Matthew 6:33 says: *But seek first his kingdom and his righteousness, and all these things will be given to you as well.*

Again, one more time, remember that your daily quiet time, your devotions, your time alone with God is essential in this process. This is the way you can continue in daily asking God to guide and help you.

3. It is sustained by Volunteer Accountability (Accountable)

This is honesty lived out in front of others. Bible study groups, small group accountability, or Christian  friends should keep each other accountable.

4. It is rewarded by Righteous Obedience. (Attitude)

Doing what God says is the right thing to do. Listening to the still small voice within you. And listen friend, You have got to want to live out this fruit of goodness (integrity).

Deuteronomy 30:19-20 says: *This day I call heaven and earth as witnesses against you that I have set before your life and death, blessings and curses. Now choose life, so that you and your children may live and that you may love the LORD your God, listen to his voice, and hold fast to him. For the LORD is your life,*

Let us end this chapter with one last text from God's Word.

1 Samuel 16:7 says: *But the LORD said to Samuel, "Do not consider his appearance or his height, for I have rejected him. The LORD does not look at the things man looks at.*

*Man looks at the outward appearance,*
*but the LORD looks at the heart."*
The Lord is always looking at our hearts. Individually…

**Will you find favor in the eyes of the Lord?**

# Faithfulness

Greek - *Pistis*

(moral conviction, faith at work)

Every family expects faithfulness. Family is a "team" effort and requires commitment and dedication, which leads to faithfulness. Faithfulness is defined as spiritual maturity. It is the inward quality of someone who keeps his or her promises and commitments. God of course is our greatest example, but we can also learn from children and grandchildren.

Lamentations 3:22-23 says: *Because of the LORD's great love we are not consumed, for his compassions never fail. They are new every morning; great is your faithfulness.*

3 John 2-6 says: *Dear friend, I pray that you may enjoy good health and that all may go well with you, even as your soul is getting along well. It gave me great joy to have some brothers come and tell about your faithfulness to the truth and how you continue to walk in the truth. I have no greater joy than to hear that my children are walking in the truth. Dear friend, you are faithful in what you are doing for the brothers, even though they are strangers to you. They have told the church about your love. You will do well to send them on their way in a manner worthy of God.*

One great way to teach this fruit is with a continuing home study of faith and faithfulness. This will help the child to understand, on their level what faith means and what faith looks like in God's Word. Take time to share in terms that they will understand. I am talking about Intentional Discipleship. That means spending one on one time with each one in the family based on their faith need. It is seeking to understand your family members and relating to them where they are spiritually. It is faith at work in each and every situation or circumstance when you are involved with them.

One night a father heard his young daughter speaking, although she was alone in her room. The door was cracked just enough so that he could see that she was kneeling beside her bed in prayer. Interested to find out what subjects a child would bring before God, he paused outside her door and listened. After tuning in to her prayer he was puzzled to hear her reciting the alphabet: "A, B, C, D, E, F, G ..." She just kept repeating it. He didn't want to interrupt her, but soon curiosity got the best of him. "Honey," he asked, "what are you doing?" "I'm praying, Daddy," she replied. "Well, why are you praying the alphabet?" he asked. She explained, "I started my prayers, but I wasn't sure what to pray. I decided to just say all the letters of the alphabet and let God put them together however He thinks best." Have you ever felt that way? You knew you needed to pray, but just weren't sure how. You didn't know the right words. You didn't know what was acceptable to God. You wanted to know God's Will, You wanted to know the right thing to do, but you just couldn't find the right words! Don't feel bad. Jesus' best friends and closest followers felt the same way. They obviously noticed how He spoke to the Father with ease. He seemed to always have the right words to say, and his prayers were powerfully answered. He seemed to always know God's will. So, they asked Jesus, "Lord, teach us to pray."

Jesus granted their request. He gave them the blueprints that He used in prayer. The writers of the Bible recorded it and today we call it, "The Lord's Prayer." A more appropriate title would be "The Disciple's Prayer" because it was given to Jesus' followers so that they could pray with power, but it was also given to teach them how to know God's Will. This prayer model is placed right in the middle of a series of messages from the Lord Jesus that we call the Beatitudes.

Beginning in Matthew 5, these are a listing of the _attitudes_ that need to _be_ in our lives as we serve the Lord. It is faithfulness in action.

There are at least 26 specific examples there in Matthew 5 of basic principles of how to know God's will and in doing God's will. This is a great place to begin to instill the fullness of understanding faith. It is a great way to model faithfulness. One can develop personal illustrations and examples to share that relate to the family. The basic principal is this:

*You know God's will by trusting, accepting, and obeying God's word and the Spirit's direction.*

I want to use one basic part of the Prayer found in Matthew 6, and moving back into Matthew 5. Here we'll see what led to this pattern, this blueprint. We will also see why Jesus answered the disciples question with, "This, then is how you should pray" Our Father in heaven, hallowed be your name". And then that great phrase, "Your Kingdom come, Your will be done…"

When we pray; "Your Kingdom come…" what are we really asking for? *Nothing really,* what we are saying is we trust in your Lordship God. We submit to you. Your Kingdom come. You see, our walk with the Lord is not a once and for all kind of thing--it's a DAILY relationship. We need to regularly recommit our lives to God by yielding ourselves to Him as subjects in His Kingdom--the Kingdom of Grace. Affirming our commitment to Jesus as Lord and King. God really wants to reveal His will to you! Ask and it will be given to you, seek and you will find. So, what IS God's Will? It is for us to accept and obey His Word and the Spirit's direction. That was the idea behind Jesus' instruction in these beatitudes. Over and over again we hear Jesus teaching in Matthew 5:

*"You have heard it said…But I tell you!"*

Jesus was saying you have heard what is true, but I tell you what the truth is…My Will! I tell you the principal behind what is true, Jesus says. You have heard of the laws, but I am telling you how to apply them. You know the basics but let me show you how to live them. Knowing God's will is accepting and obeying His Word and the Spirit's direction. Jesus is saying...You know the law but let me share with you the reason for the law...the Spirit behind it. Let me illustrate with a more modern example of this. *You have heard it said, first come first serve*...But I tell you if you arrive at the restaurant at the same time with someone older or slower than you, don't run to the door to get your name first on the list, but show kindness and courtesy and hold the door for them. Show your faithfulness to God's principles. You see it's all in the attitude...Our be-attitudes. *Jesus is saying, when you be-gin to apply my truth (even the laws) to your lifestyle, I will be so present in your life that you will know my Will. You will know my heart. This is a true be-attitude.*

You can see why it's important to teach your children and grandchildren this quality. It has such a large effect on their overall character. They need to know how to do their duty, be true to their work, steady, trusted, adhere to the truth, and believe it.

Both of our earthly fathers, (G.S. Baldwin Jr. and Paul Tucker) demonstrated faithfulness to us. They always taught us to be faithful to our commitments. "Your word is your bond" they would say. Work hard and it will work hard for you. We were told to be good employees. I got hired at a local grocery store when I was a teenager. My father told me to work hard and do whatever the manager asked me to do. After all, I was being paid to work, and so make sure I was "faithful" to do it right. And so, I didn't cheat on my time card when others were. I didn't waste time and worked even when I could take extra breaks. It was just an example that I felt like I had to demonstrate. Now, this was what I was taught, and I must admit at times I resented it when I watched others, but after I was born again in 1973, I finally understood what that heart of faithfulness felt like. That fruit of faithfulness finally made sense. And it is a great example to set before your family. ***So How can we set this key example of faithfulness?*** As we seek to harvest our *"Fruit Flavored Family"* how can we apply truth in order to know God's Will? Let us share 3 closing principals that summarize this truth and to remind us how to apply truth so our lives will clearly say, Your Kingdom Come, Your Will be done.

## 1. Understand what is true...

*Affirm the principals of God's Word...*
*Get the Facts...from God*

Study the Word, Believe the Word, Let the Word be your Guide. 2 Timothy 3:16-17 says: *All Scripture is God-breathed and is useful for teaching, rebuking, correcting and training in righteousness, so that the man of God may be thoroughly equipped for every good work.*

## Apply what is Truth...

*Listen to the Spirit within you*

Nothing is ever just cut and dry. We must always take what is true and apply God's truth as the Spirit leads.

In every one of the examples in Matthew 5, Jesus is saying, You have heard the rules (what is true) but let me tell you how to apply them (what is truth) You can translate God's Truth by His Spirit within you.

Romans 8:26-28 says: *In the same way, the Spirit helps us in our weakness. We do not know what we ought to pray for, but the Spirit Himself intercedes for us with groans that words cannot express. And He who searches our hearts knows the mind of the Spirit, because the Spirit intercedes for the saints in accordance with God's will. And we know that in all things God works for the good of those who love Him, who have been called according to His purpose.*

## 2. Add Jesus' Grace to the Truth

*Give people what God has given you…His grace, mercy and forgiveness.*

Always, do the right thing. Don't wait on others, just do what is right. Live out the Grace of God.

Jesus said here in Matthew 5:23-24: *Therefore if you are offering your gift at the altar and there remember that your brother has something against you, leave your gift there in front of the altar. First go and be reconciled to your brother, then come and offer your gift…*

### Individually, we must do what is right!

So for you and your family what do you need to ask the Father for? Are you seeking God's Kingdom, God's Will in your family? Even if you don't know the right words to say, Pray and ask Him. The Spirit will translate. Let God know your heart, come near to Him right now.

Let's look at some specific examples of faithfulness.

*1- Read the Bible to your children, and grandchildren and pray with them.*

The Bible is full of stories of men and women who were faithful in times of difficulty. Those stories can help your children to begin understanding the importance of faithful behavior. How does God feel about it? Why it that important? How does God reward it? What happened to those who were unfaithful? The ultimate example of faithfulness is Jesus Christ. Spend some time lingering on Him and His faithfulness for a picture of perfection in this area. One of the things that makes His sacrifice so great was His willingness to be faithful no matter the cost. We have tried to emphasize Christ in all that we do here. People fail, but He does not. We want our children to know that and value Him. When the time comes that my children must face something challenging, I want them to know they can turn to Him, and He will be faithful to stand with them. I want them to know He is faithful to forgive and will be faithful to keep them. Since salvation comes by grace through faith, we want our children to have a very clear understanding of what it means. They can only see it perfectly personified in Christ. God's faithfulness is important to answered prayer. Let them see God's character traits in everyday practical applications. Keep a record of your prayer requests and answered prayer. I still do this in my journal and even have shared that specifically with my children and grandchildren. Connect those prayers to Bible verses about God's promises. Talk about those you are praying for who show faithfulness in difficulty. They will see God's faithfulness with their own eyes.

I can't tell you how many times our children have seen God prove faithful in difficult circumstances. When we moved to another state in an attempt to seek God's will for our lives, in a new Church, our children saw the Lord's faithfulness. There were times when we saw unexpected blessing show up after we prayed. There were even difficult times where they had to rely on the Lord and His faithfulness. God is faithful. Let Him be the ultimate teacher.

*2- Read other stories about faithful men and women.*

Rick and Amanda Beale in their wonderful blog: *"The Fundamental Home"* give a great example. They say: "After the Bible, be sure to check out other stories of faithful men and women." Here are some books they recommend:

*Pathway Readers–* These are old Amish readers that share many different stories about men and women who were faithful. Some are difficult to read, telling stories of those who lost their lives for their faithfulness. Be sure to read ahead and decide if the stories are appropriate for your child. Even if the grade level matches up, some children are more sensitive than others.

*Classic Literature*– Many pieces of classic literature focus on doing what is right in the face of difficulty. Some suggestions (mostly for older readers, but some work great as family read-alouds) include: The Lord of the Rings series, Jane Eyre, Sense and Sensibility, and Swiss Family Robinson.

*Missionary Stories*– Missionaries have great stories to tell of God's faithfulness and their faithfulness in times of trouble. There are countless great biographies out there, so I won't even attempt to name them all. These books are definitely worth reading with your children. For little ones, try "Missionary Stories with the Millers." (Note: our International Mission Board and Home Mission Board of the Southern Baptist Convention have some great free resources on Missionaries)

*The Book of Virtues and The Moral Compass*– These are two books that I feel are a valuable addition to your collection. They are full of short stories that teach character. You may not like every story, but there are SO many good ones, and the books have the right goal. I read the books myself sometimes for encouragement.

*3- Set the example. Keep your commitments.*

It really is a matter of faithfulness. Your grandchildren and children are watching you. Have they seen you struggle to do something, but do it anyway because you said you would? Have they seen you inconvenience yourself for the benefit of others? Do you stay home from work pretending you are sick? When you make a commitment or a promise, does it mean something? Your faithfulness must be that great example for them to see and for you to define with your behavior.

Even though, I have served as a Pastor for over 40 years, I want to say, it is so important to be faithful in attendance and support at your local church. Don't miss a service unless you are providentially hindered. When we went on vacation, I would always research and find a church to worship in to set the example of that important commitment. If you are not faithful to God's house by your actions, your words will matter little.

*4- Make sure you point out other faithful people.*

Without a doubt we learned faithfulness from our fathers. I do not think our fathers ever missed work. They set the example of faithfulness in their jobs to illustrate it in their lifestyle. When you point out faithful men and women, it will support what you are teaching at home. A healthy congregation of Christian believers can be seen by the overall faithfulness of their members. Your children and grandchildren are impressionable. They are looking for examples of what you are teaching them in the lives of other people. Point it out when you see it happening.

*5- Make faithfulness a requirement*

Without a doubt this is the hardest, yet most important lesson to learn and teach. When your children or grandchildren make a commitment, require them to keep it. All you have to do is look around in our society today and the lack of commitment and faithfulness is everywhere. But, we need to make sure they see the importance of it. Our children wanted to try everything it seemed when they were growing up. From music lessons to gymnastics, from dance to every sport around and even academic extracurricular activities. They wanted to try it all. Most of the time we let them, one at a time, but required them to finish what they started. That was clear when we would begin the "new" activity.

And so they learned the importance of commitment and faithfulness.

Earlier in the book we talked about *Identity and Destiny* and teaching your children about simple integrity. I used the example of our children getting older. It is so important to keep the door open to have conversations with them about keeping commitments in relationships. It seems in our world today teaching and talking to children and/or grandchildren about relationships is tough. We know how hard it is with the internet and so much push in the media to teach purity and faithfulness, but it is possible. God says it is still our job to train them and stop them from making commitments they can't keep in order to protect them and others from the results of unfaithfulness in relationships. We strongly believe the Bible teaches that a physical intimate relationship belongs in marriage only. As the Beales say: "Your child's word should mean something, especially when they are sharing their heart with another. If we are faithful to guard their hearts, when the time comes, and your child is ready to consider a relationship, they recognize what a serious commitment they are making to the heart of another. Require your child to be faithful in word and deed."

***Faithfulness is not a fruit that will be perfected in our lives, but it is an overflow of God that is possible to demonstrate.***
Let us Pray:

*Lord I want to know your will? Let me take the truth and add grace to it. Lord Your kingdom come; Your will be done on earth as it is in heaven. Lord we want your way, Lord we want your will…We submit to your Spirit Lord…Lead us near to your heart*

***May the Lord's will be done on earth in your "fruit flavored family", as it is in heaven…Amen!***

# Gentleness

Greek - *Prautes*
(humility and gentle spirit)

This is probably the most desired fruit that every parent wants to see in their children as they are growing up. When a family has more than one child it is almost a necessity at times. Gentleness is humility shared with others. It is kindness shared with others. It is a tender attitude displayed. It is a wonderful spiritual quality displayed.

*Micah 6:8: He has showed you, O man, what is good. And what does the LORD require of you? To act justly and to love mercy and to walk humbly with your God.*

*1 Peter 5:5-7: Young men, in the same way be submissive to those who are older. All of you, clothe yourselves with humility toward one another, because, "God opposes the proud but gives grace to the humble." Humble yourselves, therefore, under God's mighty hand, that he may lift you up in due time. Cast all your anxiety on him because he cares for you.*

*Is Gentleness something one can teach? Absolutely…But, How?*

## Children visiting hospitals with us

One of the best ways that we taught our children the fruit of gentleness was by hospital visitation. You can get a list from your Church or just stop by the Chaplains office and ask if there are any persons that you all could visit. Nursing homes are another good place to visit. We would make these times special by taking each child individually and then getting breakfast, lunch or a snack together afterwards and talking about the visit. We would many times (asking our child before we went to it many times, would they mind praying for our friend). What a wonderful opportunity to share gentleness and to help our children experience this gentleness.

Another way to teach gentleness is by using their everyday childish arguments with one another or their friends to illustrate gentleness by the act of forgiveness.

Our faith as Christians is based on the concept of forgiveness. To truly understand one's Christian faith, we must understand forgiveness. Forgiveness is one of the most widely misunderstood doctrines of Scripture. It is the act of excusing or pardoning another in spite of his slights, shortcomings, and errors. This is literally accomplished by the spiritual gift of gentleness. As a theological term, forgiveness refers to God's pardon of the sins of human beings. Forgiveness is God's mercy and grace in action. It is God's gift of Reconciliation. We can use these terms, but until we understand them, we cannot receive the benefits. No religious book except the Bible teaches that God completely forgives sin.

Psalms 51:1-2 says: *Have mercy on me, O God, according to your unfailing love; according to your great compassion blot out my transgressions. Wash away all my iniquity and cleanse me from my sin....*

The initiative of forgiveness comes from God (John 3:16; Colossians 2:13) because He is ready to forgive (Luke 15:11-32). He is a God of grace and pardon (Nehemiah 9:17; Daniel 9:9). He wants to provide forgiveness in order to restore us to a right relationship with Him. Forgiveness is really how we are able to understand God's gift of salvation for us.

God can look deep into you and see your problems and needs and forgive and cleanse you. All He wants is your agreement, your trust and faith and He wants to cleanse and forgive and restore. Only Jesus can look within and know your real need.

Let me illustrate: There is a medical procedure called the PET scan. PET means Positron Omission Tomogrophy which looks at the cells in the body to detect problems and diseases. It is a scan to look inside us to see what is wrong physically. God does the same thing to our minds and hearts, our soul. He scans us by His Word and His Spirit to convince us of our need for Him.

The Psalmist cried out in Psalms 139:1-4: *O LORD, You have searched me, and You know me. You know when I sit and when I rise; You perceive my thoughts from afar. You discern my going out and my lying down; You are familiar with all my ways. Before a Word is on my tongue You know it completely, O LORD.*

Psalms 139:23-24 goes on to say: *Search me, O God, and know my heart; test me and know my anxious thoughts. See if there is any offensive way in me and lead me in the way everlasting.*

Psalms 69:5 says: *You know my folly, O God; my guilt is not hidden from You.*

So Jesus was ready to provide forgiveness for whosoever would believe and receive: the crowd, believers, whoever. Clearly Jesus had stated his purpose at another time when he said… *"I have come to seek and to save that which was lost"* …those who need His forgiveness.

Do you see what God can do today? Take a good look! Jesus came to deliver the forgiveness of God and wants us to share that forgiveness with others. No matter what use to be …you can have a new beginning. You can be born again, and start anew…Forgiven

Many of us think we can continue what we've always done and expect different results. No!…We must be born again (John 3)…Begin anew today! Only solution…Listen and Believe. Once you have…Get a Jesus Scan…

Ask the Lord to Search you and see what you need. He knows and will meet all your needs...

Will you let him scan your life today?

Will you find his forgiveness and cleansing by His gentleness?

# Self-Control

Greek – *Egkrateia*
(controlled by the spirit, temperance)

The final family fruit that seems to be self-explanatory is really not. Let me make this perfectly clear, this does not totally mean controlling yourself, but it means to be controlled or led by God's spirit. It means that one is Spirit filled and controlled by that Holy Spirit. 1 Peter 5:8-11 says: *Be self-controlled and alert. Your enemy the devil prowls around like a roaring lion looking for someone to devour. Resist him, standing firm in the faith, because you know that your brothers throughout the world are undergoing the same kind of sufferings. And the God of all grace, Who called you to His eternal glory in Christ, after you have suffered a little while, will Himself restore you and make you strong, firm and steadfast. To Him be the power for ever and ever. Amen.*

Now there are times with your children that you have to work on healthy habits of self-control...For example, Getting your teenage daughter out of the bathroom and into the car in order to be on time. Or getting the kids to put up their shoes from the middle of the floor or dishes off the tables...Whatever!

Self-control involves developing positive habits, which help one to grow into the person God created us to be one. So it takes goal setting and working to achieve them, and repetition brings habits. What are some ways to work on this?

(During most years)  Goal setting and consequences and Positive re-enforcement are the two most common in this process.

This process for the fruit flavored family begins with the Parents taking the time to think about each member of the family (including yourselves) and setting goals of character, behavior, and mutual family needs. After you have made this list you will set consequences for achieving these goals in the time frame set. Success brings the positive re-enforcement of reward with the love language best suited for the member of the family (verbal or physical). It is very important to review these with each member of the family for clarity and review them regularly as changes and needs occur. So this is a lifelong process of "practicing" this fruit. It is allowing God to build this in us.

But the Key to this fruit working in one's life is teaching by example how to listen and obey God's Holy Spirit in all things. There are dozens of Scriptures talking about this key subject. I want to be simple so you can be simple with your family. (Your discipleship calling). So I want to cover the basics tonight and then in our summary study in April, I will be more specific... Let's begin...Our text tonight is going to move from the context of Galatians in chapter 5 to the pretext of the "root of the Spirit" (root, not fruit) in Jesus's teachings in John 14-16... Remember, the fruit of the Spirit is because of the root of the Spirit. When Paul is giving us the fruit in Galatians 5, he knows the root.

Look again at the context of Galatians 5: *16 But I say, walk by the Spirit, and you will not carry out the desire of the flesh. 17 For the desire of the flesh is against the Spirit, and the Spirit against the flesh; for these are in opposition to one another, in order to keep you from doing whatever you want. 18 But if you are led by the Spirit, you are not under the Law.*

Paul is setting the context of what is the fruit of the flesh and the fruit of the Spirit. We know that God wants us to "discipline" our lives (discipleship, training, Parenting) to walk by the Spirit. The world seeks to train us to walk by the flesh. So we obey the Spirit. Paul told Timothy as he discipled him in 2 Timothy 1:7 , *7 For God has not given us a spirit of timidity, but of power and love and discipline.*

So, first let's look at the "root" John 14 (Jesus is beginning to prepare His disciples for the basics) He tells them in v. 15 ff: *15 "If*

102

*you love Me, you will keep My commandments. I will ask the Father, and He will give you another Helper, so that He may be with you forever;* [17] *the Helper is the Spirit of truth, whom the world cannot receive, because it does not see Him or know Him; but you know Him because He remains with you and will be in you.*

And so, Jesus fulfills this promise at Pentecost for the Church. And when we are born again, this Spirit indwells us. The root is there within us. So the next step is to obey the Spirit as He leads us within and through His Word of Truth.

Look back at John 14: [26] *But the Helper, the Holy Spirit whom the Father will send in My name, He will teach you all things, and remind you of all that I said to you.*

And so, again, Jesus is reminding us that God will teach us what to do and how to do it and give us His power to do it...As this discourse continues into chapters 15 and 16 Jesus gets more specific and says in 16:13-15: [13] *But when He, the Spirit of truth, comes, He will guide you into all the truth; for He will not speak on His own, but whatever He hears, He will speak; and He will disclose to you what is to come.* [14] *He will glorify Me, for He will take from Mine and will disclose it to you.* [15] *All things that the Father has are Mine; this is why I said that He takes from Mine and will disclose it to you.*

This is God's Pretext for understand the Context of this Text.

And so, finally, throughout God's Word we are given, and in our Daily Quiet Times with the LORD in prayer we are given instructions to walk in the Spirit. We just need to ask the LORD, What would you have me to do today, LORD? And obey with Spirit Control

So the root produces the fruit as we Walk in the Spirit.

Let's close with some practical examples with our families:

103

1.    Pray...Trusting God with all things...Philippians 4: beginning with verse 4 says:    *"Rejoice in the Lord always. I will say it again: Rejoice! 5 Let your gentleness be evident to all. The Lord is near. 6 Do not be anxious about anything, but in everything, by prayer and petition, with thanksgiving, present your requests to God. 7 And the peace of God, which transcends all understanding, will guard your hearts and your minds in Christ Jesus."*

<u>To Rejoice</u> is to greet one another with the joy of the Lord...that is our strength. Rejoicing can include sympathy, empathy, or just plain excitement, but the focus must always be on the Lord and what He will do for us no matter what. This must be our attitude... gentleness, patiently handling, reasonably handling, Opposite of contentiousness (argumentative) (v. 5b)   "The Lord is Near" literally means, holding your hand and squeezing to remind you that He is there and loves you. Like a parent and their child or a Grandparent and their grandchild.

Do not worry, but in everything...Pray... And make sure you keep a list with Prayer requests and dates in order to teach these truths of praying and answered prayers.

2.    Remind your family of answered Prayers...Worship and Praise and Thank God so that they are reminded of what the LORD has done. This was normal and natural with Hebrew families (feast days and family worship)

3.    Teach them of these and other examples in God's Word...Share God's truth and how He works...

Remember.... The root produces the fruit as we Walk in the Spirit. Self-control is Being controlled by the Spirit.

# "Father Knows Best"

In 1954 a new show premiered on TV with some basic moral principles. It had been on radio since 1949 and then Robert Young continued as Jim Anderson on this hit show "Father Knows Best" winning 2 Emmys…Why? It talked of real life and real situations, but with good wise solutions even in sexual issues that were covered in the show.

We have come a long way since then…or so it seems with TV and movies…We see real life situations, we are told, but no good wise solutions…Can we help? I know we don't live in the 50's with the Youngs or Ozzie and Harriet or even in Mayberry with Andy and Barney…*but principles haven't changed…*Truth is Still Truth…God's Truth

God is relational and is very much interested in who we are, what we do and how we respond to our world…(our Personal Testimonies and our personal overflow of His Wisdom) We can clearly see these thoughts through the eyes of the David in the Psalms and now through the writer Solomon, son of David in the book of Proverbs.

A proverb is a word given that directs beyond your ability. In order to attain or know wisdom and to have insight into God's worldview, there must be a reflection based on your own personal experience with God. One must have evidence that convinces…So *Wisdom* is the knowledge and ability to make the right choice at the right time… Wisdom is the evidence of God that convicts. *Wisdom is to trust God. And God's worldview comes out of Wisdom.* Wisdom here in Prov. 1:2 means to be wise in word, action, and deeds…resulting in the ability to make right choices at the right time…Consistency in this wisdom is maturity…

To do things God's way. But never forget that the prerequisite for wisdom and knowledge is the fear of the Lord (v. 7)

*If any of you lacks wisdom, he should ask God, who gives generously to all without finding fault, and it will be given to him.*

We must learn to ASK GOD FOR WISDOM. "If any of you lacks wisdom, he should ask God" (v.5). That is the basic Christian position. In other words, wisdom comes from above. It's a matter of *pure vertical sovereign grace.* It is a gift of the God and Father of our Lord Jesus Christ, and no one else.

*Wisdom* is the cry of every Father and Mother reading this. Why do we say this and what can we do to help others? Look at Psalm 25…

*To you, O Lord, I lift up my soul; 2 in you I trust, O my God. Do not let me be put to shame, nor let my enemies triumph over me. 3 No one whose hope is in you will ever be put to shame, but they will be put to shame who are treacherous without excuse. 4 Show me your ways, O Lord, teach me your paths; 5 guide me in your truth and teach me, for you are God my Savior, and my hope is in you all day long. 6 Remember, O Lord, your great mercy and love, for they are from of old. 7 Remember not the sins of my youth and my rebellious ways; according to your love remember me, you are good, O Lord. 8 Good and upright is the Lord; therefore He instructs sinners in His ways. 9 He guides the humble in what is right and teaches them His way. 10 All the ways of the Lord are loving and faithful for those who keep the demands of His covenant. 11 For the sake of Your name, O Lord, forgive my iniquity, though it is great. 12 Who, then, is the man that fears the Lord? He will instruct him in the way chosen for him. 13 He will spend his days in prosperity, and his descendants will inherit the land. 14 The Lord confides in those who fear Him; He makes his covenant known to them. 15 My eyes are ever on the Lord, for only He will release my feet from the snare. 16 Turn to me and be gracious to me, for I am lonely and afflicted. 17 The troubles of my heart have multiplied; free me from my anguish. 18 Look upon my affliction and my distress and take away all my sins. 19 See how my enemies have increased and how fiercely they hate me! 20 Guard my life and rescue me; let me not be put to shame, for I take refuge in You. 21 May integrity and uprightness protect me, because my hope is in You. 22 Redeem Israel, O God, from all their troubles! (NIV)*

Now, let's notice a few things in this Psalm: First,

### *Recognition of God (v. 1-5)*

It is so easy to say that we have acknowledged and recognized the Lordship of God almighty…our commitment as individuals and a church body to His Glory and Kingship…Our hope as Parents for our World…Always step one is Lordship, Then we are able to Affirm God's protection (v. 2b-3)

Throughout the Bible, God is seen as our Protector…

And you know when you know God is King of Kings and Lord of Lords and wants to protect His children (as any parent would) it is easy at a time like this to issue a…

Call of Hope (v. 4-5)…I will admit, I don't have all the answers, but I want what is right…God's ways….

Our hope is built and founded on nothing less than the Lord Jesus and His righteousness. Don't try to outsmart or think you know more that our LORD.

We…Either Hear and Obey God or we Hear and be controlled by the world…

### *Our heavenly Father does know Best.*

### *Reminders…to God for us (v. 6-11)*

Parents...in a lot of areas, we have been there, wish we hadn't done that (v.7) 78% of Youth in a recent survey said that their Parents were there most significant influence

Parents you need to know you have a calling that may seem to be ignored, but is valuable. You are called to Parent (Deut. 4 and 6) Teach!

Talk to your children and their friends. Teach them truth. Youth, Learn from your parents, but don't repeat the mistakes we have made. (v.8-10)

Do not cover up your sin. Practice humbly believing God's truth and obeying Him and then we can...

Call for Forgiveness (v. 11)  With a sincere heart we will receive it; we must help and support each other humbly.

Recognition, Reminders and then:

### *Rewards from God (v. 12-15)*

Notice these Revelations and Instructions as God reveals His truth and teaches us...Same survey (Barna research) reported 82% of youth said there greatest desire in life was to find and marry and only have 1 marriage partner. (Need to pray about that)  God has place His Holy Spirit within us. (another Reward from God)

Jesus said He would put His spirit in you to guide you.  (1 Corinthians 10:13 says When temptation comes your way God will provide the way of escape)

God also Confides in His children. It is His Covenant shared with us. The Promises of God are for real.

God word will Guide you in how you think and act. In  2 Tim 3:14-17, Paul says: *"But as for you, continue in what you have learned and have become convinced of, because you know those from whom you learned it, and how from infancy you have known the holy Scriptures, which are able to make you wise for salvation through faith in Christ Jesus. All Scripture is God-breathed and is useful for teaching, rebuking, correcting and training in righteousness, so that the man of God may be thoroughly equipped for every good work."*

God's word is able to keep and protect you. As we seek Him, we find the release of Life. (v.15) God's peace and God's release.

So, Recognition, Reminders and Rewards, Wow, but the R's continue. We also find:

### *Repentance, Rescue, and Refuge (v. 16-20)*

Not trying to do better, but trusting in God's promises of Accepting a Repentant heart as He is granting Peace. Basic results are given as God takes over. And it is always in God's timely action. We must change our thoughts to God's thoughts.

Phil 4:8-9Finally, brothers, whatever is true, whatever is noble, whatever is right, whatever is pure, whatever is lovely, whatever is admirable-if anything is excellent or praiseworthy-think about such things. 9 Whatever you have learned or received or heard from me or seen in me-put it into practice. And the God of peace will be with you.

Great Response…God takes over…(look at v. 20, our refuge)

### Recognition, Reminders and Rewards… Repentance, Rescue, and Refuge all leading to *Redemption in God (v. 21-22)*

1. Our Salvation
2. Renovation from God

A story is told of a man wanting to buy a warehouse building. The building had been empty for months and needed repairs. Vandals had damaged the doors, smashed the windows, and strewn trash all over the place. As he showed a prospective buyer the property, he took pains to say that he would replace the broken windows, bring in a crew to correct any structural damage, and clean out the garbage. The buyer said, "Forget about the repairs. *When I buy this place, I'm going to build something completely different. I'm not buying your building; I want to make it my building. I don't want you to make any changes...I know what is best for my new building.*"

That's God's message to us! Compared with the renovation God has in mind, our efforts to improve our own lives are as trivial as sweeping a warehouse slated for the wrecking ball. When we become God's the old life is over. He makes all things new. All He wants is the site and the permission to build. There are still some trying to "reform," but God offers "redemption." All we have to do is give Him the "property" and he will do the necessary "building." Our Father really does know what is best.

# Home Sweet Home

The word *home* has a broad range of meanings. On a personal level, it can refer to our immediate and physical place of residence; this may be a house, an apartment or condominium, a studio, boarding house, trailer park, retirement community, college dormitory or even a street corner. Home can also be descriptive of our "roots"; the place in which we grew up; our town, city, state or country of origin. Quite apart from a sense of place, home can describe the welcome and embrace of close friends or family members with whom we have a shared history. Or it can be descriptive of something for which we long; either that which we once had and desire to re-create or that which we have never experienced but ardently dream of.

Whatever definitions we use, our experiences of home, both past and present, are deeply formative. For some, *home* conjures up warm and secure memories of the past or is representative of all that is good and wholesome in the present. We are products of our homes.

Also, regardless of culture, we cannot avoid the vitality of the home as the expression of what it means to be human. Home gathers up so many of our deepest physical, emotional and spiritual needs and gives flesh to our longings and hopes for the future. In the United States homeownership, a privilege out of reach for many, is still central to the "American dream," for it stands as a monument to our drive for independence and our cravings for security and belonging.

## The Home in the Bible

In line with the Old Testament emphasis on the home as a place of protection, for raising a family, for rest, prayer and hospitality, and as part of one's legacy to one's children, the home in the New

111

Testament plays a prominent role in the ministry and mission of Jesus, and in the unfolding story of the early church.

***A Place of Spiritual Encounter.*** Though it is true that Jesus ministered and proclaimed in synagogue and temple, His favored place of ministry was the home. There was nothing that Jesus did in the name of the Father that He was not prepared to do in the home. His choice of home as a primary place of interaction is consistent with His incarnational mission; no longer was the presence of God confined to the temple, mediated by priests, but it was now the immediate and daily experience of all those who respond in faith. And that presence was encountered in the most ordinary settings, the home included.

***A Place of Community.*** As community is vital to the Christian church, so in the New Testament the home is vital to the nurture of community. Jesus spent a substantial amount of time in homes building relationships. One of His favorite activities was eating and drinking in the homes of His friends (Matthew 8:15; Luke 10:38-42; John 12:2). As we examine the life of the early church, it is apparent that the home played host more than any other venue to the development of community (Acts 2:42-47). The early church was almost exclusively a network of house churches (Romans 16:3-5; Col. 4:15; Philemon 2). Without the house as a meeting place for teaching, fellowship, worship and mission, it is hard to imagine how the early church would have found its feet.

***A Place of Ministry.*** As well as playing host to the initial process of cohesion among the earliest believers, the home was the place where the open invitation into God's kingdom was extended to all who would hear. Jesus chose to do much of his teaching and preaching Iin homes, most often while reclining at a meal table. The home was where Nicodemus came seeking truth (John 3:1-21), and it was where the crowds gathered to hear Jesus preach (Mark 2:1; Mark 3:19-21).

*A Place of Expectation.* As we examine the role of the home in the New Testament, two realities emerge. Jesus existed very much in the present. The concerns of the earthly home were not cast aside by Jesus in favor of gazing off into the future. Rather, the kingdom was understood as present and immediate, even in the home. On the other hand we have Jesus' promise that He goes to prepare a place for those who believe, a home with many rooms (John 14:2). This is part of the kingdom yet to be. It is somewhere in between these two realities that believers are called to live.

### Our attitudes today…

The question must be asked: As those seeking to integrate our Christian faith with all of life, how do we interpret God's purposes for the home, and how do we nurture our homes of today and tomorrow as places of God's presence? Apart from our recognition of our thankfulness for God's providential provision of "a roof over our heads," we should consider the following dimensions of the homes in which we live.

*A Sacred Place.* When one considers, as we have, the range of significant events to which the home played host—the incarnation, the commissioning of the disciples, the last supper, the resurrection appearances, Pentecost, the opening of the church to the Gentiles, the blossoming of the early church—it is hard to deny the home its role as a place of God's gracious and transforming presence. God's presence through the Holy Spirit can form, nurture, refresh, heal and call us, and it is ours to be experienced in the home. The Roman Catholic Church's post-Vatican II declaration of the family as "domestic church" reminds us of the sacredness of place and interaction in the home. Unfortunately, we do not often appreciate the very immediate, divine presence that surrounds us there. It is our challenge to find ways to recognize and respond to the presence and call of God, and to experience in the solitude and relationship of the home the immediacy of "God with us."

*A Place of Relationship.* The traditional bonds of community are a fragile thing in today's world. This is certainly true in the home. As our lives become more fragmented, finding time together as households is increasingly difficult. Shared mealtimes are often sacrificed in the interests of individual agendas. More often than not, the television is the gathering point in the home, an object that discourages rather than nurtures communication. If we are serious about the home as a place of interaction, then careful thought should be given to some practical matters of priority. Creating common schedules that prioritize time together is essential. Consideration could be given to the arrangement of furniture in common areas. Too often the television set is the organizing point in our living rooms. Placing it elsewhere and intentionally creating spaces that invite interaction through the simple rearrangement of chairs and lighting can make a substantial difference.

*A Place of Refuge.* While in the majority of instances recorded in the New Testament the focus of home ministry and interaction is on the open door, there are also significant instances of the house as a place to close the door on outside demands (Matthew 6:6; Matthew 8:14; Mark 5:38-43; Luke 1:24, 56). There will be times in the life of every household when it is more appropriate to focus on the healing and well-being of those within than to extend a welcome to outsiders. The various seasons of life each come with their unique challenges and demands. Our homes must serve as places of refuge, withdrawal, healing, comfort and solitude to varying degrees throughout our occupancy. Sensitivity to the changing needs of our household members must always be seen as a valid expression of our response to God's call. It is interesting to note the occasions in which Jesus directed one of those he healed to "go home" (Mark 5:19; Mark 8:22-26; Luke 5:25). He did not direct them to go and do, go and proclaim, or go into all the world: he simply commanded them to return to their homes.

114

***A Place of Mission.*** In a society that values Independence and privacy, it is perhaps our greatest challenge to stand apart, to model the welcome and embrace of the gospel where we live. The call to mission is a call to friendship. Such a call requires an open door, inviting conversation and redemptive relationship. The church is often rebuked for being more a fortress that guards the faith than an open table to which all are welcomed and where faith is shared. The home is ideally suited to model the latter. An integrated Christian faith is a key issue here too. Our place of worship and fellowship is most often separate from our place of living. In today's urban world the two can be not only in different buildings but in two completely separate parts of the city. Many today are rediscovering the New Testament house-church model (*see* Church in the Home), which helped tremendously in reintegrating these separate worlds and in re-centering the home as a primary place of mission in the world. Where possible, we can also use our homes as places for exercising hospitality to those who are traveling or on vacation, those who are engaged in itinerant ministry or home from overseas mission, and those who are temporarily homeless. While not everyone is able to have a guest room available to any who may need it, those who can afford to do so can provide one as a tangible sign of their welcoming attitude to others.

***A Place of Recreation.*** The home is a place where we can relax, be ourselves, rest and enjoy leisure. It provides opportunities for play with our families, and for creativity in the way we decorate and furnish—not necessarily an expensive affair, as the simple but beautiful and peaceful homes of many Mennonites and rural folk attest. The home is a context in which many people pursue their hobbies and crafts, extending and enriching themselves in satisfying ways that may also be beneficial to others. The uncertainty or chaos of the world outside is sometimes compensated for by the stability and order of the home. Meanwhile, the space around the house allows people to re-create the earth through sowing and planting flowers, shrubs and trees. In some cases the front and back yards of a home become a miniature Garden of Eden that signals to us our longing for the coming Heavenly Garden City (Rev. 22:1-5). In summary, the home is indeed, potentially at least, a sacred place in which the presence and purposes of God can be discovered and responded to. As a people who long for the fulfillment of God's promise of an eternal home to which we are welcomed with open arms, we have the opportunity in the present moment to experience and to be "the household of God". Our homes can be gathered up in that experience.

A Prayer of Dedication

*Lord, we enter inside this home*
*today to dedicate it for your Glory.*
*Our desire is that You dwell here in Your fullness.*
*Lord, we know that according to Proverbs 24*
*"by wisdom a house is built, and through understanding it is established, through knowledge its rooms are filled with rare and beautiful treasures". And so our prayer is that wisdom would abound here. May You always grant this family Your perspective on life's situations. Bless this Home! Establish this house with understanding and knowledge so that each room may be filled with rare and beautiful treasures of You and Your Word. We know that apart from You we can do nothing and so we ask that this house be a home touched by Your Spirit. Let this home be A Place of Refuge, A Place of Spiritual Encounter A Place of Community, A Place of Ministry, A Place of Expectation, A Place of Relationship. A Place of Mission, A Place of Recreation. A Sacred Place.*
*May Your love in all its purity, Lord Jesus, dwell here. In Your name we pray…Amen*

# What to do when you are out of Sugar

There are times for sure when "home sweet home" runs out of sugar. What we mean is things are not always sweet and cozy in a home that is at work seeking to be more like Christ. Most of the time the sugar replacement is simply, yet profoundly Communication. Norman Wright says: **"Communication is the key to marriage"**. If that is true, then it is also the key to family. When couples complain that they're not communicating, they don't realize that wives and husbands can't *not* communicate. No matter what, you are communicating. You are still communicating, even when neither of you is talking Communication doesn't require either party to utter a single sound. In fact, you can sometimes communicate louder in silence than you ever could with words.

*One study at UCLA indicated that up to 93 percent of communication effectiveness is determined by nonverbal cues. Another study indicated that the impact of a performance was determined 7 percent by the words used, 38 percent by voice quality (tone of voice), and 55 percent by the nonverbal communication.*

Imagine the following situation: You are walking down the street, when a someone knocks you down and steals your purse. You are very upset when you arrive home, and really just want your spouse's attention. However, after you finish telling your them about your horrible experience, they say nothing. Then, he starts watching the ballgame again. Is your spouse communicating something through his wordless response? You bet he is, and there's probably nothing very positive for you in that message. Perhaps your husband is saying that he doesn't really care about what happened to you. Maybe he's too caught up in his own concerns, or he doesn't know how to respond to yours. Maybe he's just too upset to talk, because he feels powerless to do anything to help you. Whatever the reason, that kind of silent communication sends a loud and clear message. He is communicating.

Communication is about a lot more than talking. Many clear and loud messages are given through attitude, facial expressions, and body language — as well as through words that are left unsaid. Communication is also accomplished physically. Your spouse can convey a message of affection by gently touching your hand or scratching your back or brushing your hair. However, if he squeezes your hand to the point of pain, that may be a very different kind of message.

To become an effective communicator, you have to pay close attention to what your spouse is telling you through their moods, attitudes, gestures, movements, and actions. The other side of this skill is recognizing the non-verbal messages you yourself are transmitting back to your spouse. You can sharpen your non-verbal communication skills by using the steps in the following thoughts.

### Watch for changes in mood and attitude

Is your normally energetic spouse suddenly down in the dumps and quiet? Is he/she distracted and forgetful in ways you haven't observed before? Is your spouse avoiding talking to you like they normally do?

These changes can be signs that there are things going on in your spouse's life (or mind) that they don't wish to discuss — at least not now. Still, you may want to say something like, "Honey, I've noticed that you haven't been your usual cheerful self lately." If they still won't address these changes with you, make a written or mental note of these shifts in behavior. Try to remain watchful of how they play out in the days and weeks to come. Watch for the right time to bring it up again. It can be difficult to see yourself with the same objectivity you apply to others. But communication is always a two-way street, especially in marriage and the family.

That's why it's important to monitor your own tone of voice, attitudes, and other nonverbal behaviors with the same sharp eye you use to observe your spouse.

### Tune into body language

Is your spouse making direct eye contact or avoiding your gaze? In general, a person who looks you directly in the eye is assumed to be forthright and truthful. On the other hand, a person who averts his eyes may not want you to know what they are thinking. You can also learn similar information by observing the way your spouse's body reacts when you ask them a question. Is their body position relaxed and open, or tense and withdrawn? In general, a person who maintains a relaxed, open bearing when you ask a direct question tends to be forthright and truthful. On the other hand, a person whose body suddenly becomes rigid may be concealing something.

### Look for signs of nervousness or tension

If you notice that your spouse is anxious in the course of conversation, note this as a possible clue that some thought or feeling is not being verbally expressed. Uncharacteristic silence or talkativeness may be another sign. The rules of interpreting body language and other non-verbal clues are well known to salespeople and others who are skilled in the art of persuasion. He or she may also be practiced in maintaining a calm demeanor and conjuring up sincere-sounding laughter at will. On the other hand, the non-verbal communications of some extremely honest people may give the mistaken impression that they're trying to deceive you. That's why it's wise not to draw any firm conclusion from any single clue. Instead, incorporate each non-verbal clue into the total picture of what your spouse is communicating.

## *Double-check the meaning of gestures*

Every gesture is a communication of some kind. But when each spouse assigns different meanings to the same gesture, it can cause friction in the relationship.

For example, a wife may call her husband at work twice a day because she wants to feel connected. However, the husband can interpret this gesture in a very different way. He may feel that his partner is checking up on him or trying to smother him. You can easily misinterpret the meaning of a particular signal. Avoid such mistakes by taking the following steps:

- If you're at all unsure, ask your partner to explain her nonverbal communication.
- After you identify the emotion that provoked the gesture, work at addressing it
  **(portions taken from: _http://www.dummies.com_)**

I want you to notice that these basic communication skills that you have learned are not new Psychological truths or something Cheryl and I came up with. These communication techniques are normal and natural, and any "dummies" (pun intended) can learn and apply. Learning to have effective communication in marriage is one of the most important aspects of marriage that a couple can work on. Before anything else, it is important to dispel the myth that your husband or wife should always now what you are thinking. This attitude can be stated as "if you don't already know what the problem is, you don't deserve to know." This is wrong! As obvious as a problem may seem it is unfair and impossible to expect a spouse to be able to always tell what the problem is. This attitude focuses on the wrong issue - trying to get your partner to guess the problem instead of trying to find a solution. Instead we should be direct and open in our communication, allowing our time and energies to be spent on resolving the problem. Cheryl and I have an understanding that if we feel something is not right, we can ask each other and not be offended by what someone "feels". The Bible teaches us "not to be easily offended." We are both wanting our marriage and family to work. So let us suggest a few helpful hints. Plan a scheduled time to talk- One of the most difficult problems when a couple is very busy is finding the time to talk. Communication takes a significant amount of time. Cheryl and I have always had a weekly time to go over our calendars and schedules. By scheduling a weekly "planning meeting" you can make sure that at least once a week each person has the opportunity to express their concerns and frustrations (make sure you talk about good things too!) God has given you 2 ears and 1 mouth. Listen twice as much as your talk. Really we need to listen more carefully than you think you need to - before moving on to discussing a solution, make sure you *really* understand what your spouse is saying.

Many times the greatest stress with communication in marriage simply comes from the feeling that you are not being heard. Your spouse wants to know you are listening. Focus on principles not positions - effective communication occurs when we learn to focus on common principles instead of differences in position. Usually we focus an argument on opposing positions ("you don't think my cooking is as good as yours" or "you think Caleb's bedtime should be at 7:00 and I think it should be at 8:00"). Instead if we can focus on the underlying principles of the issue at hand (such as being healthy or making sure your children are well rested) they are almost always the same for both people. Simply recognizing shared principles makes negotiating a solution easier because you feel like you are both on the same team. In this case you can look for win-win situations where both people feel like they are satisfied with the solution. Always take time to Pray –Besides getting God's opinion and getting information from His Word, the simple, humbling act of asking for help from the Lord softens both of our hearts and makes communication easier. Praying together as a couple and asking the LORD to help you so that you are inspired to find creative solutions to the issues at hand will go a long way in bringing communicative peace. As you work to improve your communication in marriage, you will find strategies of your own. It may help to write them down, so you have some additional ideas for conflict resolution in the future. Regardless of what strategies or ideas you use to improve communication it is *always* better to address problems through communication than to bury them thinking that they will go away eventually - they won't! Talk it out in a way that is supportive and loving whenever necessary. God will amaze you.

# Vital Signs

How is your family doing? What is it really like?

In order to build a strong family, you must first take your "vital signs". Just like checking your pulse, heart rate, and temperature, the family needs to check what is normal, natural and healthy in a "spiritual" sense. With our world trying to define and re-define what is "normal, natural and healthy" the "fruit flavored family" must set their own norms. Using Biblical standards and realities within the context of Christian principals, we need to check our "vital signs" regularly to make sure we are all right. The "vital signs" for the strong family are almost like a process. They take work!

### Our relationship with God.

The first vital sign is our *relationship with God*. God must be kept at the very "heart" of the family at all times, in all situations, and in every circumstance. Parents must focus on letting their daily life and routine shine with God at the center. Our relationship with God through the Lord Jesus Christ must be the basis for our identity and destiny. It provides the flow of our legacy. It is what we naturally pass on to our family. One definite way to make sure this happens is to determine your priorities. Make a determined decision to put Christ at the center of all you do in prioritizing your time and commitments. In doing so, we will help our family see the world from God's perspective. For example, always plan to attend Church on Sundays. Do not make this optional, but from the very beginning make this a priority. Even when you are on vacation, find a place to spend in Worship together as a family. By doing so you are setting a lifestyle    commitment that will be remembered. Always do so    with an attitude of prayer and excitement. Knowing that God will speak to us as we seek Him, you can be assured that the Lord will communicate with your family wherever and whenever you desire His direction.

When the Lord is at the center of the family, and parents are taking the lead in instilling Godly values, then creativity becomes a necessity. Parents need to think of ways to teach about God's Love, joy, peace, patience, kindness, goodness, gentleness faithfulness, and self-control in many different ways and with many specific daily examples.

Our values flow naturally from our faith walk and become the very basis of this "value clarification." Let your family seek your relationship with God as being real and natural. Encourage your family to ask questions about that relationship, remembering that all questions are valid as each one searches for their own clarity in their own values. Keep your number one priority on the family's personal relationship with God through salvation in the Lord Jesus Christ and everyone other area with fall into place.

### Your relationship with one another

The second vital sign to check is your *relationship with one another.* How do you say to your family that they are the second most important relationship that you have? It begins by meeting the "needs" of your family. Understanding and focusing on physical, emotional, and spiritual needs helps one get ready for the work ahead. But, the family must take these concepts of needs and put them into natural, recognizable teaching models.

We must use the normal, everyday situations and circumstances to teach the "fruits of the Spirit" to our family. Love can be demonstrated in showing one another that you truly care. From birth and beyond parents can show that they care in attention, affection, and appreciation. Keeping a good check on what are

124

needs and wants, the "fruit flavored" parent can begin to teach by just doing what comes naturally. But as the family continues to grow, this natural teaching becomes more objective. We have to set goals and realize that we are in competition with worldly standards and fleshly desires.

This is the time where we have to again set our priorities. We have to make time to pay attention. This means special time for each one as an individual as well as in our family group. This means applying the principals of "fruit flavoring" to each one in the family according to their needs and personalities. The same is true when we think of affection. A hug, a pat on the back, and a loving word are all ways to begin to show affection for the family.

Everyone loves to be complimented. This is something we can strive to do each and every day for each and every family member. The final and most needed way to show we care is by appreciation. Every person has a tremendous need to be appreciated. Verbal compliments, notes of admiration, and gifts to thank someone are all good ways to begin this path of mutual appreciation. We need to talk about it as a family and do it regularly to one another. In a society that tends to be driven by performance, we must take the personal approach to appreciation. The family member must be affirmed that God has placed them in "this family" for a special purpose and plan. Performance is not primary; it is simply an expression of seeking to do one's best. It too should be noticed and affirmed, but not focused on. The family is special because they are "who" they are, not because of "what" they accomplish. We all want to be appreciated for "who" we are as a member of the family. Each person needs to hear and believe that.

Christmas 2006 was a great time for our family to display this truth to each other. Our family had gathered with Cheryl's full family (Mother, Father, Sister's and children) and went to the beach together. One evening we all gathered in the den for a time of affirmation. One by one each family member would sit front and center in front of the family. We would each take turns affirming the best qualities we had seen displayed in each person's life. We even took time to write these down and give them to the person afterwards. This took a lot of time but was worth the effort to show love and care.

Bonding is a term that is often used only to refer to the early years of parenting. Bonding is when a parent and child share intimate time together resulting in a physical, emotional, and even spiritual connection. Bonding for the "fruit flavored" family is something that is essential to work on continuously. This takes time, effort, and commitment also. Knowing a person's "love language" is vital to this effort.

Can't you picture it? You return after a few days away from home, and your children rush to meet you. One smothers you in hugs and kisses, another jumping up and down asking if you brought her anything. As the Father you take your coat and bag upstairs, while Mom tells the children she missed them and is so glad she is finally at home.

Demonstrated in this common scene are four very different ways of showing love. Understanding your friends' and family's love languages can be very helpful as you seek to serve and love them. For me, it has been encouraging to see that, while I have a different love language than everyone else in my family, if I understand other's love languages, I can better serve and understand them.

"Love Languages", first discussed by Dr. Gary Chapman in his great series of books on the subject are simple, yet profound to understand. Let us review them for you.

This is not an exhausted treatise on the subject, but simply a summary. If you are interested check out more about this subject from the books recommended in the "tools" section. Dr. Chapman has a great website to help you.

If you've ever felt "unloved", it may be because your loved ones are not showing love in a way you easily see, but recognizing the various ways of expressing love is a tremendous help. Christ alone perfectly loves each of us and fulfills every need we have for acceptance and understanding. But may our goal be to love as He has.

## 1. Words of Affirmation (Language of Words)

My first love language is Words of Affirmation. This is when you need to hear those three little words, "I Love You", a lot. Also words of appreciation, words of encouragement, words that build up. If you don't hear them, you don't feel loved. This is also how you express your love to your mate, your children, your friends. You want to hear and say those words of Love and affirmation.

We all like to hear an encouraging word now and then, but some people need that "I love you" on a daily basis. This doesn't necessarily mean that they have a low self-esteem, though that is a common misconception. Quite simply, words of endearment and praise are as vital to some people as water and bread. I know that for me (Garry), having someone tell me "I love you," is just about the best thing in the world. I know that being told how good I did on something makes me work even harder. This is definitely my love language. Hearing encouragement, promises of loyalty, love, and, as the title suggests, is affirming to me. For those of you who are the "Words of Love" type, you probably give this love more than you receive it.

Since it is your "love language" you are sensitive to give it away to others, whether they want it or not. Perhaps you like to talk things through thoroughly and analyze conflicts down to the bone, much to the dismay of the other types, who would just as soon put the situation behind them without spending an hour discussing it. But remember if you are feeling unloved, that all the affirmation you can ever need is found in the Bible. There should be more than enough passages of love and loyalty to lift you up. The key to showing love to this type of person is to say the assumed, even if you think it is a given. The people who long to hear "I love you," and "I'm proud of you," will be amazingly encouraged by those simple words.

Words are powerful. Whether the power comes from actual words or the tone of voice in which they were said, it is there. Although everyone needs verbal affirmation in their life, a person who speaks the language of Words of Affirmation, feels a lack of affirmation very keenly. Likewise, positive words are "honey to their soul." Our words of appreciation and honest compliments are powerful communicators of love. They are most easily expressed in simple, straight forward affirmations, like, "What a beautiful dress!" or "Thank you for doing the dishes for me" or, "I really do appreciate it that you took out the trash without being asked." Describing an art project brought home by a child: "Oh those clouds are round and fluffy. The barn is a pretty shade of red. And look at those tulips! Yellow is my favorite color. What a beautiful picture!"

Helping a wife feel valued as a mother and homemaker: "Honey, I saw the time you took to help Jeremiah after you dealt with making supper and cleaning up even though you were tired. I appreciate that. You were patient with him even when he didn't get it the third time. Your patience and diligence continues to make me so happy I married you." Husbands, you have just hit a home run!

To me (Garry) when Cheryl offers loving encouragement when I look tired and offering to let me sit down and rest instead of demanding me to do something for her is such a blessing...I love it.

On the flip side, words that are spoken with a nasty tone or those dripping with sarcasm or negative words, will be felt most sharply by someone who speaks the language of Words of Affirmation. There is great power in our words. We can speak with life, or we can speak and cause "death". Impact from our words spoken in haste with anger and elevated tones is great. They bring damage to a marriage or great pain to a child's molding soul. This is why Scripture devotes so much time to informing us of the dangers of the tongue.

The old saying rings true with Words of Affirmation people: "If you don't have anything nice to say don't say anything at all." We should be trying to compliment and encourage those we love, whether they speak this particular language or not. However, if you know or are discovering that your loved one thrives on compliments and verbal affirmations then, open up your mouth and speak the love they need to hear. If you are to the point in a certain relationship and feel that there is nothing good you can say to your troublesome person, you'll need to be creative. Scripture tell us in Philippians 4:8 to think about whatever is noble, pure, lovely, admirable, excellent or praiseworthy. There is something about the other person. Ask God to reveal something admirable to you.

## 2. Quality Time ( Language of Quality Time)

Does your mate, children or friend always want your undivided attention? Do they get upset when you don't stop what you are doing when they want to talk? Do they want to spend time alone with you without you doing the dishes or the needlework or tinkering with your latest hobby. All of us enjoy spending time with loved ones, and who doesn't feel treasured when you have an in-depth discussion, or fun game with your family? For some people this is their primary way of receiving and expressing love. For some it is the hardest to give, as it requires, in some ways, more of yourself than others. It is perhaps easier to hug someone than spend an hour with them, but true Christ-like love is willing to love in all ways.

As nice as it is to know what your language is, more importantly, strive to learn other's languages, and earnestly love them. Jesus perfectly loved everyone by healing, teaching, touching, caring, but most of all, by that act which we can never truly appreciate. His death is our life, and because of His love we can and must love others.

The key to loving is Quality Time and Conversation. Whether you are talking with them or doing something with them that they enjoy, this time equals love. Their motto is a lot like Nike's: Just Do It… With Me!

The Quality Time language can be broken down into two parts: quality conversation and spending quality time together doing something. Although both are based on the concept of spending Quality Time with a person, one needs to do something together and the other needs to talk. A Quality Conversation Person needs undivided attention when you talk with them. They need to know you are talking with them not the TV, baseball game, the boss or mother on the phone. They want you to talk with them. A Conversation Person needs your undivided attention when they talk, and you listen. While you listen, you need to be a keen listener for their feelings so you can offer nurturing conversation when it's your turn to talk.

A quick "Hi. How was your day? simply isn't adequate for someone whose love language is Quality Time . They want to talk about the day, how they feel about the day, how you feel about their day and then, they want to know about your day and how you feel about your day and then, they will tell you how they feel about your day. This will definitely be a conversation that takes a good amount of time. A great thing is to do is make an 'appointment' to listen later in the evening, during or after dinner or before bed to sit down and talk. Not only will your Quality Conversation person know you care enough to listen, but they will also know you make the time to be with them.

Dr. Chapman suggests these tips for becoming a better listener when you are in love with Quality Time Conversationalist:

1. Maintain eye contact when talking.
2. Don't listen and do something else at the same time
3. Listen for feelings. "I feel like..."
4. Observe body language.
5. Refuse to interrupt.

The other language of Quality Time is those who want to spend time with you doing things. These fine folks long to do things with you while they have your undivided attention. This is what makes them feel special and loved. The definition of Quality Time often differs for men and women. Naturally, because women are more verbal, they often want to talk over coffee or while taking a walk. However, men and boys might be content to do something, but not necessarily talk. A game of pickup basketball, cards or changing the oil on your car may be just what's needed to qualify for Quality Time.

If you love someone that is always asking you to do something with them: a board game, a bike ride, a walk, a movie, a trip to the mall, anything that involves doing and going with them, and most times them alone, chances are their language is Quality Time. So get to it! The only thing a Quality Time Person needs is to be with you and have your undivided attention.

### 3. Receiving Gifts (*Language of Gifts*)

Now don't panic on this one. Gifts do not mean that you have to go out and spend buckets of money on them, they just like little remembrances. A flower you picked on the way home, a pretty stone, a card, something you made, just so it is from you.

This language could easily be seen as a more fleshly desire. It may seem selfish. But let's look at it from God's point of view. He too gives gifts to His children. Why? Out of His amazing love for us. I do not see anything wrong with the occasional thoughtful gift given as a sign of love, in hopes of encouraging another and aiding their spiritual growth. Some people are gifted to show love in this way. Learning to give as God gave—out of love.

Giving gifts has always been used as a way of conveying love. We do it at Christmas, birthdays and weddings. We fulfill needs and we give small pleasures. We make people happy when we give gifts. Everyone likes to receive gifts, but if you find yourself riding high for days because your husband brought you home a bouquet of flowers or your friend dropped by with a tin of homemade cookies, then chances are you are a Gifts Person.

Gifts People love to give gifts too. My (Garry) mom was a perfect example of this. She loves to buy people gifts. She says it's just a way to show her family how much she loves them especially at Christmas.

It is not that Gifts People are greedy and want a lot of things. Gifts People like the idea that someone thought enough of them to get them something - anything.

In times of crisis or hardship, your time could be the most valuable gift. Things like offering to babysit someone when something unexpected happens or silently sitting with a person when a loved one has passed away are both good examples. This type of gift can be the sweetest thing a Gifts Person has ever known.

When little or big tokens are few and far between, Gifts People don't feel loved. You don't have to break the bank to keep a Gifts Person feeling loved. Be creative. A unique vase from a yard sale to match new wallpaper, a silly scarf that will go with a treasured jacket from a thrift stores, wild flowers from your drive home or a favorite candy bar from Wal-Mart all say that you were thinking about your Gifts Person.

## 4. Acts of Service (*Language of Service)*

This is when you do things for the one you love. This could be mowing the lawn, building a house, keeping the house spotless, washing and cleaning the car. You serve the one you love in many ways and expect them to serve you back.

I need not expound to you the significance and necessity of serving the Body of Christ. This love language is an intense form of that need to serve. I have a friend who is constantly cleaning, writing sweet notes, taking time to teach someone something, reading to a sick child, being a peacemaker, or helping someone with something.

However, to love someone in this way, you must die to your personal wants and selfish ambitions. That is the hard part. But those whose language is acts of service need you to serve them. Doing a chore for someone unasked may be a wonderful opportunity to love.

Although this language seems fairly self-explanatory, sometimes it can be difficult. For the Acts of Service language, you express your love by serving. You listen for the hints they drop about the things that they would like done and then you try to see those things get accomplished. This is the language of people who don't need to be told they are loved, they want (and need) you to show them. Little Acts of Service are how they know they are loved.

To some, this means the dishes are done, laundry washed, folded, ironed, put away, grass is mowed, trash is out, dinner is done, a babysitter is on the way and groceries are being brought in as we speak. You bake a cake, or some cookies and hearts are melting. You can offer to massage some aching feet or run to the post office and your Service Person is put in your hands!

Heaven forbid an Acts of Service person to marry someone who is not that tidy - then we have serious problems! An Acts of Service husband knows he is loved when he comes home from work with dinner simmering on the stove, a cake in the oven and a tidy house. However, if the wife hasn't gotten her act together yet and dinner is not done and the dishes are piled high, the husband may take that to mean that his wife just doesn't care about the things that make him happy – even if this isn't the case! She may love him to pieces and tell him all the time. But telling is not good enough. He needs the dishes done! If you love the Acts of Service person, just like the other languages, it may be necessary for you to go the extra mile.

You may need to do some strategizing about things you can do that you know they will appreciate. You may need to listen to their complaints and see if you can head them off at the pass next time. A number of years ago, Random Acts of Kindness became very popular. It's a day where everyone is encouraged to do nice things for others they know, as well as complete strangers. When you live with and love an Acts of Service person, you need to be doing random and regular acts of service every day to let them know just how much you love them. Just make them "intentional" acts of kindness.

## 5. Physical Touch (*Language of Touch*)

This is when you like to touch. A hug, a pat on the arm, a stroke on the cheek, a back scratched will satisfy this love language. Know an adorable little girl who thrives on cuddles and hugs? Or perhaps you are the type of person who needs that goodnight hug and kiss from your parents. Several in our family have this love language. They just loved to be touched.

Back rubs are the evening ritual for many in our family. We know this language very well. For the people in your life who enjoy that hug or hand squeeze, make a special effort to show them you love them in the way they can most easily recognize. Whether it's the three-year-old you teach in Sunday School or an older sibling, physical touch is one of the best ways to show Christ's love. Remember 1 Corinthians 13 and keep your heart and motives pure.

It's been rumored a person needs 7 hugs a day to stay healthy. How many have you had today? Physical Touch is any gentle and loving touch: a hug, caress, a hand on your shoulder, a foot rub, holding hands, a kiss on the cheek, running your fingers threw someone's hair... The examples are endless.

Babies left alone in orphanage cribs have died because there was no one there to hold them, touch them and coo to them. All people need to be touched. We can hug good-bye, we can lay on hands & pray over someone, we can massage. Touching is therapeutic! We need to be touched. For some people this is their language above all other ways of speaking love. They would rather be held, touched, poke caressed and kissed. Without extra special and deliberate touching, the love of these people withers and dies frightfully quickly.

Dr. Chapman says if you're having trouble figuring out what love language an adult is, look at how children express their language.

Physical Touch people appreciate all kinds of touch.

Keep in mind that physical touch involves tender, innocent, ticklish, and sensual touches as well as boyhood wrestling, noogies and 'mindless' caress. So go on and tickle, caress, poke, tousle, hug or kiss. Your Physical Touch Person will feel your love for them by touching them!

### Your relationship with the world.

*The third and final "vital sign" to check for the health of your family is your relationship with the world.* This brings the greatest commandment that Jesus gave us full circle: Loving God, loving self *(family)*, and loving your neighbors.

*…"Of all the commandments, which is the most important?" "The most important one," answered Jesus, "is this: 'Hear, O Israel, the Lord our God, the Lord is one. Love the Lord your God with all your heart and with all your soul and with all your mind and with all your strength.' The second is this: 'Love your neighbor as yourself.' There is no commandment greater than these." (Mark 12:28b-31 NIV)*

It is important to stay involved in our world, so that our children see the servant heart of Jesus in us. This can be anything from volunteer work at the Church to neighborhood ministry projects. The list is almost limitless as to how and what one can get involved in. I do suggest beginning by asking your Pastor how you can be involved in "Mission" opportunities. He will be more than happy to direct you into this type of involvement.

*Just reading through this book has felt like "work", I am sure, but… It is the most important work that really matters in this lifetime. God has called you to "disciple" your family. You have some basic tools. We will be praying for you! God Bless you as you begin!*

## _Additional "Tools" and Resources for the "Work"_

_https://www.christianparenting.org/about/_ Listen to the "about" comments at this great website: As believing parents we know how important it is to raise our children with love and focused attention, giving them a picture of God's love for them every day. But most days we're stretched too thin to do more than the status quo. That leaves us feeling reactive instead of proactive, never growing into the parents we know we were created to be. And the highlight reel we see online only leaves us feeling more hopeless and inadequate, seeing a picture of perfection we'll never measure up to. We created Christian Parenting to give you the practical and spiritual help you need, on as many platforms and in as many ways as possible. Hundreds of thousands of parents are being transformed by our resources every day, and it's helping people set aside perfection and actually grow into the perfectly imperfect parent they were made to be.

_www.christiangrandparenting.com/_ is a new website create by Sherry Shumann and Deborah Haddix and focusing on some great suggestions for grandparenting. This is a great resource.

www.focusonthefamily.com/parenting/7-essentials-for-grandparenting-your-grandkids/ is a great website created by James Dobson's _Focus on the Family_ and provides many great resources for parenting and grandparenting. Still the classic site.

www.5lovelanguages.com This great website by Dr. Gary Chapman gives you resources for all your "love language" education. Check it out.

www.fruitflavoredfamily.blogspot.com This is our blogspot that we began in 2011 and then revamped it in 2016 while teaching and now in 2023 we are re-launching it with weekly ongoing Marriage enrichment helps. Check it out also please.

# Family Connections and Final Reflections

Many families today seem to be disconnected. They are out of touch with each other in understanding, needs and direction. And with a loss of connection, there is no communication. It is an age-old problem. One writer put it this way...

"Our youths love luxury. They have no manners and contempt for authority. They show disrespect for their elders and love to talk instead of listen...They contradict their parents and gobble up food and tyrannize their teachers"....Many of us may think, Yea that sounds like today, but it was actually written by Socrates in 400 BC.

Family connections are an age-old problem. And with divorce rates so high, and the nuclear family disappearing the problem of a family connection grows even more rare.

So What can be done? Is there a solution...Can we reconnect with the family? I really believe we can...I want to finish this book with some final reflections about family connections. To do this accurately, let's begin by looking at Colossians 3 and see what the Bible says...

*Wives, submit to your husbands, as is fitting in the Lord. 19 Husbands, love your wives and do not be harsh with them. 20 Children, obey your parents in everything, for this pleases the Lord.21 Fathers, do not embitter your children, or they will become discouraged. 22 Slaves, obey your earthly masters in everything; and do it, not only when their eye is on you and to win their favor, but with sincerity of heart and reverence for the Lord. 23 Whatever you do, work at it with all your heart, as working for the Lord, not for men, 24 since you know that you will receive an inheritance from the Lord as a reward. It is the Lord Christ you are serving. 25 Anyone who does wrong will be repaid for his wrong, and there is no favoritism. 4:1 Masters, provide your slaves with what is right and fair, because you know that you also have a Master in heaven. (NIV)*

The Bible gives some basic Family Instructions on how to make the family unit function effectively. Our own personal selfishness or self-centeredness may get in the way or disagree with God's truth because it doesn't fit in with our lifestyles, but God's word is absolute truth. It is clear! For family connections to be a reality each one of us must do it God's way. It is not demanding that others do it but accepting God's standards and truths and applying them to your life personally. Let's begin.

### v. 18…1. Wives must decide to Submit to their husbands as is fitting to the Lord…

It is hard to teach this because I know the controversy based on misinterpretation and misunderstanding, but here goes…. "Submit" is not a synonym for bondage. Submission is always voluntary. "Wives, submit to your husbands, as is fitting in the Lord actually contrasts with the plight of women in the ancient world. William Barclay writes:   Under Jewish law a woman was a thing; she was the possession of her husband, just as much as his house or his flocks or his material goods were. She had no legal right whatever. In Greek society a respectable woman lived a life of entire seclusion. She never appeared on the streets alone, not even to go marketing. She lived in the women's apartments and did not join her menfolk even for meals.

But, the domestic rules given here in Colossians were vastly different from those of the day. Wives here were addressed *equally* with their husbands, something *radically new*. Also, both husbands and wives had duties—not just the wives. They were both

139

admonished "in the Lord." The context of this phrase begins in verse 17, which makes it clear that the totality of their lives was to be regulated by it. This brought a vast dignity to both men and women. They were both under the Lordship of Christ as equals. All of this was immensely elevating to women and would raise their positions greatly in the ancient and modern world.

At the same time, within the marital relationship these words established a definite *order*. As F. F. Bruce says, Paul "does hold that there is a divine instituted pattern in the order of creation, and in this order the place of the wife comes next after her husband."[5] However, this <u>does not</u> suggest (here or anywhere else in Scripture) that the wife is naturally or spiritually inferior to the husband, or vice versa....*For example*... There is an order in the Holy Trinity, and yet equality. Orthodoxy teaches that the Son is simultaneously *equal* to the Father and *submissive* to him. Likewise, *equality* and *submissiveness* can coexist in human relationships, including the marriage relationship."

AT Robertson's Greek Word Studies says it this way,

What God means by submission is <u>*order, cooperation, relationship, and partnership*</u>—that a husband and wife are to walk *together*, *hand in hand*, throughout life. Everybody of people—even when the body is only two persons—must have a leader who takes the lead in plowing through the wilderness of the world and its trials and temptations and difficulties. Between the two, wife and husband, one of them has to be the primary leader. God's order for the two is that the husband take the lead. The Christian wife, in obedience to her Lord, accept the authority of her husband's leadership, authority, and control...Thus we move to the next verse...

## 2. Husbands must decide to love their wives...

Verse 19 says "Husbands, love your wives and do not be harsh with them." Here the commandment to men is just as radical as that to women. The novelty of such a command must have struck the Colossian Christians with great power. Husbands were commanded to love their wives! My children would say, "Well Duh", which means that is clear for everyone. But the command here was to love with *agape* love, which involves unceasing care and loving service for the wife's entire well-being. The Christian requirements for a husband's love for his wife was way beyond the formal domestic requirements of the day.

A parallel passage (Ephesians 5:25-33) helps us understand the love that is called for here, especially verse 25: "Husbands, love your wives, just as Christ loved the church and gave himself up for her." Thus, this radical command to love is only fulfilled when a husband loves his wife in imitation of Christ's love.

A husband's love must first, then, be *incarnation.* Genesis 2:24 anticipated this high call when it said, "a man will leave his father and mother and be united to his wife, and they will become one flesh." The idea is something of a *mutual* incarnation. With this ancient truth in mind Paul wrote in Ephes. 5:28-29, "In this same way, husbands ought to love their wives as their own bodies. He who loves his wife loves himself. After all, no one ever hated his own body, but he feeds and cares for it." This is a high call and may seem impossible. But it is possible to love our wives as we love our own bodies. Practically, this means that the husband must do all he can to understand the world of his wife. Loving our wives as Christ loved the Church also involves *intercessory prayer.* Christ so perfectly participates in our lives that he perfectly prays for us. We must pray for our spouses in intimate detail, not just with a blanket blessing. We must praise God for her strengths and lay her needs before him. She needs detailed prayer for what she faces each day, for how she relates with the children, for her interaction with the neighbors, for her many duties, for her insecurities, for her challenges. One thing we suggest strongly is to keep a journal and write down your prayer requests for one another and date it along with the answers and the dates. This will build both of your faiths.

We have seen two radical calls. One call is to wives: *submission*. The other is to husbands: to *love* as Christ loves. These cannot be read in isolation; they go together. It is absurd for a Christian husband to expect submission of his wife if he is not radically loving her; likewise, it is wrong for a wife who is not submissive to demand such love. These brief words give us the pattern for fullness in Christian marriage connections—full love, full commitment, full exchange, full blessing. Whether we are just beginning as newlyweds or far along in years, let us have no other goal than having the best marriages possible! This is God's perfect intention for us.

A third ingredient for many of us here to make those family connections involves the children…again though it becomes their choice for a healthy family…So for children…

3. **Children Obey your parents in everything, for this pleases the Lord…** *Families connections require order in the house.*

Obedience is a key concept of God's Word…Jesus even said, If you love me you will obey me. Obedience is not just a regulation we follow. It is function that we live out. If love is abounding then everything that is done is for the benefit of the entire family. Jesus observed , If a son or daughter asks his father for a fish, he will not give him a snake, or a piece of bread a stone…So it is God's direction to obey…Many problems solved. Disobedience leads to disunity and discord. Problems… But I want you all to notice one other point  *This pleases the Lord…*Wow…

142

Do you want God to be pleased, above yourself? Obey your parents in everything…This…Pleases God…Now I know that is sometimes hard if your parents are always on your case…so Paul adds one last thought…

Especially for us Father's if we are going to accept this order…For we must set the pace…

**4. Fathers, do not embitter , or they will become discouraged….*I think one of the main problems today, begins with the head of the household*….**

Fathers, we have a job to do…Setting the example….

Notice that the advice is primarily to "Fathers," the reason being that this would be more typically a father's sin.[4] The husband is naturally away from the children more than the mother and is thus less in touch with their feelings and more prone to false judgments and unwise direction. The specific sense of the Greek word is to irritate one's children either by nagging or putting them down.[5] The parallel in Ephesians 6:4 says, "Fathers, do not exasperate your children" and has the same idea of irritating them through perpetual fault-finding.

Parents, fathers, discipline is to be given, but so is encouragement. Obedience is to be nurtured by love and praise. We must never cause our children to "lose heart."

Another kind of father who exasperates a child is the one given to irritability or grouchiness. Most people maintain a false face at work because they *have* to do so. Only the Lord knows how many children "lose heart" because their fathers have hard days. But there is another ingredient found in this text…look at v. 22 and following into ch. 4.v 1.

*. 22 Slaves, obey your earthly masters in everything; and do it, not only when their eye is on you and to win their favor, but with sincerity of heart and reverence for the Lord. 23 Whatever you do, work at it with all your heart, as working for the Lord, not for men, 24 since you know that you will receive an inheritance from the Lord as a reward. It is the Lord Christ you are serving. 25 Anyone who does wrong will be repaid for his wrong, and there is no favoritism. 4 Masters, provide your slaves with what is right and fair, because you know that you also have a Master in heaven. (NIV)*

Paul's teaching here was accompanied by a great amount of tension, for several reasons. Primary was the amazingly vast extent of slavery and its dehumanizing nature. Ancient historians estimate that there were some 60,000,000 slaves in the Roman Empire, or about one-half the population. Because of this, work was considered below the dignity of the slave-owning Roman free man. Practically everything was done by slaves, even doctoring and teaching. Though there were some relationships between masters and slaves, basically the life of a slave was not very happy.

In our society today I am sad to say we are disconnected by necessity. The Husband will spend 40 plus hours away from his family. Children almost the same in school, and Wives thus, whether at work or at home the same amount. This amounts to over 1/3 of your daily time away from one another, not counting your sleeping hours which is another third. This means we have 1/3 of each day with a possibility of being together. Is it possible to build family connections while away from one another in this way. It seems like no, but God shows a way in these verses…

### So what is the Key? Practice your Faith and Commitment to the Lord in order to build Consistency.

The first step is making a decision of what is most important in your life. We must be the same at work or at home. This is a clear notice to the Workers. (Slaves in this culture) We are to be consistent in how we work and live. Some of you may be saying , What's changed? Why can't we still obey? And what are some basic ways to do this?

Notice 3 words in v. 22:  Trustworthy, Faithful, Dedicated.

In Luke 16 Jesus shares an example of dealings with a worker and his master…notice in the final thoughts Jesus says….Luke 16:10-12

*"Whoever can be trusted with very little can also be trusted with much, and whoever is dishonest with very little will also be dishonest with much. 11 So if you have not been trustworthy in handling worldly wealth, who will trust you with true riches? 12 And if you have not been trustworthy with someone else's property, who will give you property of your own?*

This means simple integrity and wise stewardship. We have got to be Trustworthy, Faithful, and Dedicated with a sincerity of heart. Basically, you have to want to family. You must make that decision. It doesn't just happen naturally. Reverence (respect) for the Lord is commanded in God's Word. So we must develop these character traits by practice, then v.23…Committed, setting the example

Titus 2:9-10 says:

*9 Teach slaves to be subject to their masters in everything, to try to please them, not to talk back to them, 10 and not to steal from them, but to show that they can be fully trusted, so that in every way they will make the teaching about God our Savior attractive.*

Jesus taught his disciples in John 13:15-17 by saying…

*15 I have set you an example that you should do as I have done for you. 16 I tell you the truth, no servant is greater than his master, nor is a messenger greater than the one who sent him. 17 Now that you know these things, you will be blessed if you do them.*

145

Looking further at these instructions…we also see in v24…*The Lord will Reward*. With a mindset that I am serving the Lord in all things.

Paul shared the same truth with the Ephesians when he said…Ephesians 6:5-8

5 Slaves, obey your earthly masters with respect and fear, and with sincerity of heart, just as you would obey Christ. 6 Obey them not only to win their favor when their eye is on you, but like slaves of Christ, doing the will of God from your heart. 7 Serve wholeheartedly, as if you were serving the Lord, not men, 8 because you know that the Lord will reward everyone for whatever good he does, whether he is slave or free.

And finally in v. 25 we will learn Accountability.

*25 Anyone who does wrong will be repaid for his wrong, and there is no favoritism.*

Paul even emphasizes this stronger in 2 Corinthians 5:5-10

*5 Now it is God who has made us for this very purpose and has given us the Spirit as a deposit, guaranteeing what is to come. 6 Therefore we are always confident and know that as long as we are at home in the body we are away from the Lord. 7 We live by faith, not by sight. 8 We are confident, I say, and would prefer to be away from the body and at home with the Lord. 9 So we make it our goal to please him, whether we are at home in the body or away from it. 10 For we must all appear before the judgment seat of Christ, that each one may receive what is due him for the things done while in the body, whether good or bad.*

And Paul doesn't just stop with workers. He talks about bosses, supervisors, the master in charge in ch. 4:1

*4:1 Masters, provide your slaves with what is right and fair, because you know that you also have a Master in heaven.*

You see when we practice our faith and leadership all the time whether at work, at home, in public, and in the church, we are allowing God to use us to prove His plan is working for the obedience. It is filling the "fruit flavored family" wonderfully and effectively. This applies to us all, Students, Workers, and Homemakers, Family Connections are developed over time and in every area of your life. And you bring home these frustrations and hurts. So we are called by our LORD to live His Wisdom out in obedience. But you must answer one last question as we end this book.

*What is God calling you to do for His glory?*

How can we know the right way?...the truth...the absolutes that will direct us. The Bible is an up-to-date map of life. Even though it may contain some ancient paths, they are the roads, maps, and road signs that direct us to eternal, abundant life. Does it change never, but do the roadblocks, detours, construction, etc. get in the way...yes. You see the location is the same...but how to get there is a journey. We know that Family Life is A Significant Journey. How can we apply the "fruit flavored family" along this significant journey. We must learn to seek this truth in today's language so we can get there. And every week we all encounter people on their Significant Faith Journey that also are looking for answers and directions. They are wanting some clear directions. There is only one solid direction, God and His Word. We have outlined that in this book, now let's summarize with some final suggestions.

Now... In order to obey and follow a map you have got to understand the basics of the map. What the symbols represent, and how to read it. If we are to understand God's word as a map we must do the same.

*Proverbs 3:5-6* says: *Trust in the Lord with all your heart, and do not rely (lean) on your own understanding; 6 think about (acknowledge) Him in all your ways, and He will guide you on the right paths (make them straight)* God's word gives us a clear direction on how to read the map of Life...It begins with

## 1. Trust...(Believing God and His Word)

We must begin by trusting in the map we are using. We must be assured that it is accurate. Absolute truth. We can trust God and His word in all situations and circumstances of life. Whatever comes our way, we can and must trust God. Our own understanding may be based on feelings. God's word is truth. God has got it all under control. You don't have to try to figure out what is going on. Trust God!

*Aware that God is Aware... Mathew 10:29-31*

*29 Are not two sparrows sold for a penny? Yet not one of them will fall to the ground apart from the will of your Father. 30 And even the very hairs of your head are all numbered. 31 So don't be afraid; you are worth more than many sparrows.*

God knows all that is happening around us. Be aware.

*Assured that God has all the Answers...Ps. 145:17-19*

17The LORD is righteous in all his ways and loving toward all he has made. 18The LORD is near to all who call on him, to all who call on him in truth. 19He fulfills the desires of those who fear him; he hears their cry and saves them.

God already knows what to do...So I must

*Adjust my Attitude toward God...Mark 4:35-41*

148

*35That day when evening came, he said to his disciples, "Let us go over to the other side." 36Leaving the crowd behind, they took him along, just as he was, in the boat. There were also other boats with him. 37A furious squall came up, and the waves broke over the boat, so that it was nearly swamped. 38Jesus was in the stern, sleeping on a cushion. The disciples woke him and said to him, "Teacher, don't you care if we drown?" 39He got up, rebuked the wind and said to the waves, "Quiet! Be still!" Then the wind died down and it was completely calm. 40He said to his disciples, "Why are you so afraid? Do you still have no faith?" 41They were terrified and asked each other, "Who is this? Even the wind and the waves obey him!"*

By awareness and assurance, I can adjust my attitude.

God and His word will begin to make sense when you approach it seeking to understand it. And with full assurance and confidence , you can make it.

**So #1 Trust …(Believe God and His Word)**

**2. Obey…(Do what God says to do in His Word)**

Obedience is to follow God's directions as He commands. In Proverbs 3….it says…He will guide and direct your paths. This means to appoint, command, put in order. And if we follow His directions, this is obedience. When you obey…God directs…this is the main thing we must do in our lives.

Let me illustrate. While we were Pastoring in Kentucky we lived through Tornado 2000. The toughest part was cleanup. When I preached during these days, I was able to apply God's Word and lived by a simple standard. What I learned from God's word about cleaning up after storm (no matter what kind)…was...

1st …Put emotions aside (not deny, but delay)

2nd…Plan your Work (prayer, wisdom)

3rd….Work your Plan (one step at a time…consistent)

If you are to see your "fruit flavored family" flourish practice Proverbs 3:5-6

So 1. we Trust,( we make it through the storms of life by trusting God)

 2. We obey, (We clean up our lives and put them back in order by obedience) and finally

3. Have Faith (Trust and obey God in every situation) Not matter what comes your way believer God wants you to be successful.

Too many Christians think that their faith is to help them escape storms, when God has given us faith to make it through storms, to clean up afterwards, and get ready for the coming storms. Jesus said it this way to His disciples in John 16:33…."*I have told you these things, so that in me you may have peace. In this world you will have trouble. But take heart! I have overcome the world.*"

Listen to a very clear illustration of how found in Matthew 7:24-29

*24"Therefore…(referring back to v. 15ff) so he is talking to believers….Therefore… everyone who hears these words of mine and puts them into practice is like a wise man who built his house on the rock. 25The rain came down, the streams rose, and the winds blew and beat against that house; yet it did not fall, because it had its foundation on the rock. 26But everyone who hears these words of mine and does not put them into practice is like a foolish man who built his house on sand. 27The rain came down, the streams rose, and the winds blew and beat against that house, and it fell with a great crash." 28When Jesus had finished saying these things, the crowds were amazed at his teaching, 29because he taught as one who had authority, and not as their teachers of the law.*

Having Faith is putting your trust in God and your Obedience in His word into practice every day.

Trust and Faith is founded on the Rock of Obedience

Practicing your Faith…Don't blame God for anything, but realize He is in control of everything…one writer put it this way…"Fear God , and you'll have nothing else to Fear"

One can live on other's advice, or your own feelings. (sand) or one can live on God's truth…His Word…(Rock)

Insurance is a waste of money till you need it, but Assurance…God's wisdom practiced is never wasted

Proverbs 3:5-6 can be a life verse for us all.

*Trust in the Lord with all your heart, and do not rely (lean) on your own understanding; 6 think about (acknowledge) Him in all your ways, and He will guide you on the right paths (make them straight)*

### Family Basics are Basic…

*As a believer we need to Review and Evaluate our lives daily in our Quiet Times How are we doing?*
*We can review and evaluate at the same time with a regular fruit inspection.* In this book we have discovered the Bible uses the word Fruit many times in a most descriptive way to describe actions. God used it specifically in the Creation Story to focus on commands to the family. *In Genesis 1:28–29, God blessed them; and God said to them, "Be fruitful and multiply, and fill the earth, and subdue it; and rule over the fish of the sea and over the birds of the sky and over every living thing that moves on the earth." Then God said, "Behold, I have given you every plant yielding seed that is on the surface of all the earth, and every tree which has fruit yielding seed; it shall be food for you;*

*God is giving the family 2 commands and a reminder here.*

1. Be Fruitful and 2. Multiply… and then I give you fruit for food (to remind us)

Mosaic law decreed that fruit-bearing trees be regarded as unclean for 3 years after planting, as the Lord's in the fourth year, and to be eaten by the people only in the fifth year. This preserved the health of the tree against premature plucking, gave God his due place, perhaps commemorated the entrance of sin by forbidden fruit and certainly inculcated self-discipline. Fruit trees were so highly valued that for many centuries thereafter, even during the bitterest wars, special efforts were made to protect them (*cf.* Dt. 20:19–20).

Children are sometimes spoken of as the fruit of the body or womb (Dt. 28:4; Ps. 127:3). The term fruit has also inspired a large number of metaphorical uses, involving such phrases as the fruit of the Spirit (Gal. 5:22); fruit for God (Rom. 7:4) and for death (Rom. 7:5; *cf.* Jas. 1:15); fruit of the lips (*i.e.* speaking, Is. 57:19; Heb. 13:15); fruit unto holiness and life (Rom. 6:22); fruit of the wicked (Mt. 7:16) and of self-centeredness (Ho. 10:1); fruit in season (*i.e.* true prosperity) fruits of the gospel (Rom. 1:13); of righteousness (Phil. 1:11; Jas. 3:18); fruits which demonstrate repentance (Mt. 3:8; *cf.* Am. 6:12). The unfruitful works of darkness are contrasted with the fruit of light (Eph. 5:9) 'The tree of life with its twelve kinds of fruit' (Rev. 22:2) some regard as 'a sacrament of the covenant of works, and analogous to the bread and wine used by Melchizedek (Gn. 14:18) and to the Christian Eucharist (Mt. 26:29) in the covenant of grace. More probably it is a symbol of abundant life (Jn. 10:10).

The Hebrew word for Fruitful is *"Parah"* which means to Bear Fruit. With its continued literal and metaphorical use throughout the Word of God, *it seems that God was wanting the family to grasp the*

152

*"fruit flavoring" that He wanted to add to the mix. The physical and spiritual touch that the family can bring to the plan of God lived out.*

Be obedient, Bear Fruit …and don't forget!

*Bearing Fruit is a simple overflow of God in us.*

When Jesus spoke these truths in John 15, He was preparing His disciples to continue the business of the Kingdom. He calls it the "Masters' Business" and what He learned from His Father in v. 15 He is clearly telling them what they are to do as believers. *Not optional, but appointed and commanded obligations.*

Strong Words, but Jesus was giving the Disciples the Keys of Kingdom living…the most important task of believers.

Jesus wanted them and us to get real, so He uses real life *examples* that they would understand. So Jesus is saying that we are called to bear fruit. This is our job, not to make fruit, but to bear it, We are appointed and commanded. And fruit has a purpose:

1.  To meet needs…to provide food and drink
    Fruit is always grown for someone else's benefit

2.  To produce seeds…produce more fruit

3.  Reflects character of the tree.

In broad terms, a fruit is a structure of a plant that contains its seeds. The term has different meanings dependent on context…such as apples, oranges, grapes, strawberries, When we look into our own lives,

Are we seeking to produce, Is there a seed of desire within our lives? Do we want to? The seed of promise Is there. If you are a believer, the seed is there, waiting for you to tell someone, invite someone, share with someone. *If you are for real, then obey…*To remain means to Abide, to stay closely connected. Do what the Lord Commands, stay connected to the vine. Be available to share, to produce the fruit of His Spirit *Leave the rest to God*. So simple but so true, Fruit on the vine doesn't have to worry about the weather, Just trust the Vinedresser…the gardener… What Jesus was saying is this, If you have Jesus in your heart, for real, Obey and love one another, and let God Love through you. And God will bring the results. We are chosen and appointed by God to bear fruit…Accept His love into your life, See His Love come out of your life. Know He will Love through your life. You can't do it on your own, Apart from Jesus, you can do nothing. Let Jesus use you today. Let the LORD help you become the *"Fruit Flavored Family"*.

# End Notes and Bibliography

*(Helpful resources used in writing this book.)*

All Scripture (unless otherwise noted) is quoted from: The Holy Bible, *New International Version*, Copyright 1973, 1978, 1984 by International Bible Society.

Balswick, Jack O., and Judith K. Balswick. *A Model for Marriage: Covenant, Grace, Empowerment and Intimacy.* Downers Grove, IL.: IVP Academic, 2006.

_____. *The Family: A Christian Perspective On the Contemporary Home.* 3rd ed. Grand Rapids, MI.: Baker Academic, 2007.

Billy Graham Evangelistic Association, Decision Magazine. *"Raising Children in a Godless Age."* November 2014.

Brandt, Henry R., and Kerry L. Skinner. *Marriage, God's Way.* Nashville, TN.: Broadman & Holman, 1999.

Bridges, Jerry, *The Fruitful Life: The Overflow of God's Love through You.* Colorado Springs, CO: NavPress, 2006.

Carter, Elizabeth A. and, McGoldrick, Monica, eds., *The Expanded Family Life Cycle: Individual, Family, and Social Perspectives*, 3rd ed., Allyn and Bacon Classics in Education. New York: Pearson Allyn & Bacon, 2005.

Chapman, Gary D. *The Five Love Languages: How to Express Heartfelt Commitment to Your Mate.* Chicago: Northfield, 1995.

_____. *The Marriage You've Always Wanted.* Chicago, IL.: Moody, 2009.

Curran, Dolores. *Traits of a Healthy Family: Fifteen Traits Commonly Found in Healthy Families by Those Who Work with Them.* New York: Ballantine Books, 1984.

Fiorenza, Francis Schüssler, and John P. Galvin. *Systematic Theology: Roman Catholic Perspectives.* Minneapolis, MN: Fortress Press, 1991.

George, Timothy. *The New American Commentary.* Vol. 30, *Galatians.* Nashville, TN: Broadman and Holman, 1994.

Girgis, Sherif, Ryan T. Anderson, and Robert P. George. *What Is Marriage? Man and Woman.* American ed. New York: Encounter Books, 2012.

Hanson, Merri-Lee. *"Rites of Passage." Van Gennep and Beyond, School of Lost Borders,* available from: www.schooloflostborders.org, Internet; Accessed 26 February 2015.

Harley, Willard F. *His Needs, Her Needs: Building an Affair-Proof Marriage.* 15th ed. Grand Rapids, MI: Fleming H. Revell, 2001.

Hughes, R Kent, and Barbara Hughes. *Disciplines of a Godly Family.* Rev. ed. Wheaton, IL: Crossway Books, 2004.

Kuhatschek, Jack. *Peace, Overcoming Anxiety and Conflict.* Grand Rapids, MI: Zondervan, 1991.

Montesquieu, Charles de Secondat, and Thomas Nugent. *The Spirit of Laws.* Complete ed. Cosimo Classics. New York: Cosimo, 2011.

Montgomery, Dan, and Katie Montgomery. *Compass Psychotheology: Where Psychology and Theology Really Meet.* Albuquerque, NM: Compass Works, 2006.

Moo, Douglas J. *Galatians*. Baker Exegetical Commentary on the New Testament. Grand Rapids, MI: Baker Academic, 2013.

Moon, Gary W, and Benner, David G. eds., *Spiritual Direction and the Care of Souls: A Guide to Christian Approaches and Practices*. Downers Grove, IL: InterVarsity Press, 2004.

Nock, Steven L., Laura Ann Sanchez, and James D. Wright. *Covenant Marriage: The Movement to Reclaim Tradition in America*. New Brunswick, NJ: Rutgers University Press, 2008.

Nouwen, Henri J. M., Christensen, Michael J., and Laird, Rebecca. *Spiritual Direction: Wisdom for the Long Walk of Faith*. San Francisco: Harper San Francisco, 2006.

Olshin, David. *"Boys will be Boys, Rites of Passage and Male Teens,"* posted on October 3, 2009, available from: www.youthspecialties.com/articles/boys-will-be-boys-rites-of-passage-and-male-teens. Internet; Accessed 26 February 2015.

Olson, David H L., and John D. DeFrain. *Marriages and Families: Intimacy, Diversity, and Strengths*. 4th ed. Boston: McGraw-Hill, 2003.

Packer, J. I., *Knowing and Doing the Will of God*. Ann Arbor, MI: Servant, 1995.

Piper, John, *The Surpassing Goal: Marriage Lived For The Glory Of God*, in Biblical Foundations for Manhood and Womanhood, ed. Wayne Grudem. Wheaton, IL: Crossway, 2002.

Riggs, Barbara A., and Cynthia Benn Tweedell. *Marriage and Family: A Christian Perspective*. 2nd ed. Marion, IN: Triangle, 2010.

Rubio, Julie Hanlon. *A Christian Theology of Marriage and Family*. New York: Paulist, 2003.

Sandford, John, and Paula Sandford. *Restoring the Christian Family.* Lake Mary, Fla.: Charisma House, 2009.

Schwartz, Mary Ann, and Barbara Marliene Scott. *Marriages and Families: Diversity and Change.* 7th ed. Upper Saddle River, NJ: Pearson Prentice Hall, 2013.

St. Clair, Barry. *Ignite the Fire: Kindling a Passion for Christ in Your Kids.* Colorado Springs, CO: Chariot Victor,1999.

Trask, Thomas E., and Goodall, Wayde I. *The Fruit of the Spirit: Becoming the Person God Wants You to Be.* Grand Rapids, Mich.: Zondervan Pub. House, 2000.

Wilkinson, Bruce and David Kopp. *Secrets of the Vine: Breaking through to Abundance,* anniversary ed., Breakthrough Series. Sisters, OR: Multnomah, 2006.

Wright, H. Norman. *Communication: Key to Your Marriage.* 2nd ed. Ventura, CA: Regal Books, 2012.

# About the Authors

**_Garry Baldwin_** has Ministered and Pastored Churches in North Carolina and Kentucky since 1976. He holds degrees from The Citadel, Southeastern Baptist Theological Seminary and various post-graduate degrees and honors. Dr. Baldwin has led conferences in Family Relationships, Church Growth and Development, and Church Leadership. Currently Dr. Baldwin just retired as Pastor of Midwood Baptist Church in Charlotte, North Carolina in August 2023 and now serves as the Department Head for Pastoral Studies at Charlotte Christian Theological Seminary.

**_Cheryl Baldwin_** is a 1976 graduate of the University of North Carolina at Greensboro in Early Childhood Education; Cheryl has been involved in Education leadership since 1976. She helped start a Christian School, two Preschool Development Centers, and taught and trained leadership all over the world. She has been involved in the development of various ministries at Midwood Baptist Church including the Parents Day Out Preschool Ministry which is over 10 years old. She continues to serve as a consultant in Preschool Ministry and in retirement ministers to her children and grandchildren.

**_The Baldwin's have 3 Grown Children and 4 Grandchildren_**